AN INFLATION PRIMER

by Melchior Palyi

The Tyranny of a prince in an oligarchy is not so dangerous to the public welfare as the apathy of a citizen in a democracy. — Montesquieu, Spirit of the Laws.

HENRY REGNERY COMPANY
CHICAGO   1961

The Institute for Philosophical and Historical Studies, Inc., 64 East Jackson Boulevard, Chicago 4, Illinois, is a non-profit corporation organized, among other purposes, to encourage and disseminate studies that are calculated to add to the understanding of philosophy, history, and related fields and their application to human endeavor. Books in the various Institute series are published in the interest of public information and debate. They represent the free expression of their authors and do not necessarily indicate the judgment and opinions of the Institute.

© Copyright 1961 by Henry Regnery Company
Library of Congress card number 61-10743
Manufactured in the United States of America

PREFACE

Except for minor corrections and additions, this study was completed in June, 1960, and delivered at the end of the following September. Publication having been delayed for over three months, the last chapter was rewritten to take cognizance of the "gold crisis" that has lately come to the fore.

The idea to write a little book of this nature was suggested to the author nearly two years ago by the publisher, Mr. Henry Regnery. For many useful hints and observations, I am greatly obliged to Mr. Marion R. Baty, editor of the Economic Trend Line Studies (Chicago), and to Dr. Walter E. Spahr (New York). My sincere gratitude is due, especially, to Mr. Philip M. McKenna, President of the Kennametal, Inc., of Latrobe, Pennsylvania, for his inspiration and generous help.

Chicago, January 17, 1961   MELCHIOR PALYI

CONTENTS

I. INFLATION'S SYNDROME.............. 1
   Galloping and Creeping Inflation
   "Legalized Robbery"
   Inflation Defined
   Creeping Inflation—A Preview
   Where Does the Inflation Stand?

II. THE *Modus Operandi* OF INFLATION... 10
   Productive Credit—Monetizing Real
      Purchasing Power
   Inflationary Monetization
   Liquidity—by Inflation
   The Central Engine of Inflation

III. THE FOUNTAINHEADS OF INFLATION.... 18
   The Money-Printing Automat
   Managed Money—the One-Way Road
   Inflation by "Debt Management"

IV. THE VICIOUS SPIRALS 28
   The Parable of the Horse
      and the Trough
   Cost-Push Inflation?
   Built-in Inflation

V. RIDING ON THE INFLATION CREST 39
   Spreading the Inflation
   The Fallacy of Built-in Stabilizers
   The Productivity Debate
   Labor Disincentives by Inflation
   Productivity and Capacity to Pay

CONTENTS *(continued)*

VI. THE CONSUMER (AND TAXPAYER) BE DAMNED 48
    Who Pays the Bill?
    The Pot Calls the Kettle Black
    Profit Inflation

VII. THE "PHILOSOPHY" OF INFLATION 56
    Opportunism Versus Principles
    "Mind Your Own Business"
    Perpetual Prosperity without Tears
    The Rationale of the Cycle
    Progress or "Growth"?

VIII. CREEPING INFLATION AND INTELLECTUAL HONESTY 71
    How Much Is a Little?
    Cutting the Dog's Tail Piecemeal
    Power Versus Freedom
    Must We Follow the Kremlin?

IX. CREEPING INFLATION'S BALANCE SHEET: THE LIABILITIES 84
    Progress by Inflation
    The Liability Side
    Borrowing a Living Standard
    "People's Capitalism"

X. THE BURDEN OF THE NATIONAL DEBT ... 98
    Is It a Burden on the Nation?
    The Economics of the Debt
    Fiscal Legerdemains
    Falsifying the Bank Balance Sheets

CONTENTS (continued)

XI. THE CURSE OF THE DEBT............110
    The "Rationale" of Inflation
    Fictional Finance and Monetization
    Expanding on Overdraft
    Debt Liquidation
    Creeping Inflation's Suicide

XII. THE DOLLAR ON THE SICK BED.........119
    "Good as Gold"
    The Sick Balance of Payments
    Dollars in Oversupply
    Can the Balance of Payments
      Be Redressed?

XIII. THE SAD PREDICAMENT OF THE FOOL'S
     PARADISE 128
    Heading for Insolvency
    Erosion—How Much Longer?
    At the End of Creeping Inflation's
      Rope

APPENDIX..............................135
BIBLIOGRAPHY 144
INDEX.................................147

I
INFLATION'S SYNDROME
GALLOPING AND CREEPING INFLATION

In the summer of 1923, the German inflation was rapidly heading toward the grand finale: total repudiation of the currency. As an instructor in a Berlin college, this writer drew a *monthly* salary that had been raised from an inflated 10,000 marks or so in early 1922 to 10,000,000 marks by July, 1923, and the whole amount was being paid twice a month; then, once every week; then once each day. The next step to meet the skyrocketing living costs was to pay us twice a day, in the morning and in the afternoon.

Just after 5 P.M. one day in late August, 1923, I was walking down the staircase of the school, carrying the day's second haul of ten million marks (the day's first paid for a modest lunch), when the professor of physics overtook me. "Are you taking the streetcar?" he asked. "Yes," I said. "Let's hurry. The fare will be raised by 6 P.M. We may not be able to pay it."

Galloping inflation threw the German economy into virtual chaos and demoralized large segments of the German people. Adolf Hitler was the ultimate outcome. But at least it did not last long.

Presently, we are living almost a lifetime with creeping inflation that is supposed to go on indefinitely—without accelerating. Admittedly, the galloping kind is pernicious. Not so, we are being assured, the creeping type; the advantages of the latter far outweigh whatever unfavorable repercussions there may be. Anyhow, we have (allegedly) no other choice but to continue what we have been doing for the last two decades or longer, and let the dollar's purchasing power slide further —at a leisurely rate.

"LEGALIZED ROBBERY"

According to the U.S. Bureau of Labor Statistics, the index of (average) consumer prices has risen from 1939 to mid-1960 from 100 to 209—the purchasing power of the dollar declined from 100 to less than 48. This is what a former French premier, Paul Reynaud, called "legalized robbery." Indeed, it is confiscation without compensation. The victims are deprived of their purchasing power. This is "robbery" on a national scale—a surreptitious levy on liquid income and wealth, raised in a haphazard fashion, with no regard for ability to pay, no respect for the rule of law, for equity and justice. It penalizes the saver, especially, and the honest producer, while the lucky operator and the political manipulator may reap unearned rewards. It is legalized, of course, the government itself being the culprit.

INFLATION'S SYNDROME

Formal legalization does not confer justice by any economic or ethical standards. The free-enterprise system stands on the pillar of the inviolability of contracts; this pillar is weakened as the value of money is impaired.

"Legalized robbery" is a universal feature of counterfeit money, one created by government fiat. It is the product of deliberate, arbitrary measures, not of economic processes. It generates in the political arena, from which the effects spread to the market place. The powers that rule over fiscal and central banking policies determine, in effect, whether there will be inflation, how much, and for how long.

INFLATION DEFINED

To be sure, not every rise of prices qualifies as inflation. Sporadic oscillations should be disregarded. Nor is it of interest in our context if the rise has been brought about by an expansion of gold mining or gold imports. Price levels may rise under the purest gold standard, but to a limited extent only. Gold is a very scarce commodity; paper is not. "Gold-inflation," if any, is self-correcting; paper inflation is limited only by the total collapse and repudiation of the currency.

It is the inflation of the money volume—paper currency and bank deposits—that creates the fact and maintains the expectation of a disproportion between the total supply of goods for sale and the total amount of purchasing power people have and are ready to use. Hence the definition; Money-creation is inflationary when the additional purchasing power has no counterpart in goods and services people want to buy—when too much money chases too few goods.

In other words, inflation is a condition of the economy in which a rising volume of created money brings about rising production costs, higher prices, and increasing costs of living.

Inflation tends to "feed on itself." The longer it lasts, the stronger the *expectation* that it will continue. People borrow, spend, and speculate more freely than they otherwise would. The money circulation is accelerated, the average dollar does additional work, and prices are boosted additionally.

CREEPING INFLATION—A PREVIEW

The purchasing power of the dollar is measured by a weighted index number of retail prices related to a base period. The measure is far from exact; it is merely an indication of the trend, or drift. And "drift"—upward—our living costs have, year after year since 1933, almost without interruption. At that, the consumer price index does not account for everything we buy. It is tailored to the household budget of the "average" worker who spends little on books, colleges, travel, hotels, and similar luxuries; the cost of personal services bought by the consumer is understated, too. And no price index can do justice to changes in the quality of goods we buy or to the price effect of trade-ins.

An idea of what inflation means is conveyed by the table.

DETERIORATION OF FIXED-DOLLAR-VALUE ASSETS
HELD BY INDIVIDUALS*

Year	Total Assets (billions)	% Depreciation of Purchasing Power of Dollar	Loss of Purchasing Power of Assets (billions)
1940	$126.7	1.25	$ 1.6
1941	133.3	10.02	13.4
1942	140.7	7.25	10.2
1943	162.9	2.89	4.7
1944	197.7	2.16	4.3
1945	237.0	2.13	5.0
1946	272.5	15.40	41.9
1947	283.2	9.29	26.3
1948	290.9	1.32	3.8
1949	297.0	2.05	6.1
1950	306.3	7.34	22.5
1951	313.3	4.02	12.6
1952	328.5	0.68	2.2
1953	346.8	1.14	4.0
1954	366.7	0.81	3.0
1955	383.4	0.23	0.9
1956	399.6	3.09	12.4
1957	418.2	3.31	13.8
1958	437.6	1.22	5.4
1959	459.6	1.61	7.4
		Total loss	$201.5

*Compiled by American Institute for Economic Research, Great Barrington, Mass.

The fixed-dollar-value assets include mortgages, bonds, bank deposits, savings accounts, the paid-for insurance and social security claims, etc. held by individuals. And these savings of individuals account for about 60 per cent of the annual capital accumulation. In twenty years they lost a total of $201.5 billion! By that much, the debtors grew richer—or did they really? We shall see. This much is certain: the debts of consumers, businesses, farmers, and municipalities grow faster than the respective incomes. The financial position of all debtor categories is worsening year after year. The same holds for the biggest debtor, the national government. Its obligations and commitments have accumulated *much* faster than did the debt "relief" brought about by currency depreciation. The average interest charge on its outstanding debt instruments has risen in ten years from 2 per cent to over 3 per cent. Balancing the budget becomes increasingly difficult, and the Treasury has to dig ever deeper into the taxpayers' pockets.

That brings us to a most significant aspect of this inflation of ours, different from those of the past. The Civil War, for example, was financed largely by inconvertible paper money—greenbacks. Taxes were negligible by present-day standards. Now, only a fraction of the governmental expenditures is covered by incurring new debt. By far the greater portion of the public revenue is raised by taxes which suck up more than 25 per cent of the national income. The tax burden falls largely on the lower-middle-income brackets and on business. One consequence is the difficulty for the average citizen to protect his fortune against the inflation without resorting to hazardous and dubious practices. What the government gives the speculator by windfall profits and the debtor by reductions in the real value of his debt, the government takes back by taxing away much of inflation's dividends—and a great deal of the victimized savers' incomes. (Hence the fact that the proportion of income saved was lower in the 1950's than in the 1920's.)

Another consequence of heavy taxation is the "creeping" character of the inflation process, a novel departure in the sad history of inconvertible paper money. Heavy taxation takes a great deal of zest out of the inflation. However, the operating cost of the government, the greatest buyer of goods and services, tends to rise faster than its revenues. In any case, *the larger the deluge of paper money, the higher the taxes* to forestall the "gallop" and to correct alleged or real inequities. The net result is that people pay more and more taxes in order to lose each time a fraction "only" of their incomes' purchasing power.

Whether taxes are negligible or high, there is at least one similarity between the "gallop" and the "creep." The one produces trillionaires and quadrillionaires in untold numbers. The other causes millionaires to pop up from here and there —lucky speculators, happy tax-avoiders (evaders), and ruthless manipulators. The German trillionaires were literally wiped out when the currency was stabilized. As to the bulk of our new rich, it will be interesting to watch where their millions of dollars will end up.

WHERE DOES THE INFLATION STAND?

The inflation of the last twenty-odd years is a matter of record. But are we in danger of having more of the same? As this book goes to press, the highest monetary authorities, including the head of the International Monetary Fund, assure us that the inflation is over. (Have we not heard that before?) Vested interests in and out of Congress actually tell us that "deflation" is what we are up against. Of course, it all depends on what one means by such words as inflation and deflation.

What matters is the present and prospective behavior of the cost of living. In the twelve months ending June 30, 1960, the cost of living went up again by about 2 per cent. Industry's labor costs keep rising even faster; at that, some of the recent wage boosts have not yet produced their induction effects on prices. Few experts doubt that the wage level is still directed upward, or that such development would have no effect sooner or later on the cost of living. And the decisive indicator is the money supply, the number of dollars available for purchases. It has been rising year after year, boom or recession, at an *average* rate of 6 per cent or higher. The most imaginative statisticians do not figure on much more than 2 per cent average annual increase in the physical volume of salable goods and services. The disproportion is patent, and this is responsible for the prospect of *future* price inflation.

Year	Money Supply* (billions)	Year	Money Supply (billions)
1929	$ 55.8	1957	$227.7
1945	150.8	1958	242.6
1955	216.6	1959	246.6

*Cash in circulation plus net demand and savings deposits.

II

THE "MODUS OPERANDI" OF INFLATION

Money originates in one of two ways. One way is by depositing gold, the value of which is credited to the depositor on a bank account. However, the bulk of the nation's "purchasing power" stems from credit extended by banks,[1] be it by loaning funds or by purchasing securities (bonds).

PRODUCTIVE CREDIT—MONETIZING REAL PURCHASING POWER

As an illustration, let us take a simple case: A New Orleans merchant sells $100,000 worth of cotton to a mill in Manchester, England. The buyer, whose credit is guaranteed by an English bank, promises to pay as soon as the consignment arrives. The seller needs money right away and borrows from his local bank by discounting the bill signed by the buyer. His deposit account is credited with, say, $75,000. Presently, he may draw checks on the new deposit. Apparently, $75,000 had been "created" by a stroke of the pen, as it were. Add all similar transactions occurring at about the same time, and a great deal of purchas-

THE "MODUS OPERANDI" OF INFLATION

ing power is being put in circulation. Should that not cause a rise in prices?

Nothing of the sort will happen through this type of transaction. The new credit does not generate inflationary expectations; it is of the self-liquidating kind; the backflow in 90 days is assured, and the deposit will be wiped out. Actually, as it is being granted, a maturing loan may be paid back. The total money supply need not be affected at all, or for a very short time only. Even if it is affected, the additional dollar balance is matched, value for value, by the actual sale of new products. The credit is noninflationary because it has grown out of an honest-to-goodness business transaction.

The bank did not really create purchasing power; the bales of cotton sold were the real purchasing power that was not available at once to the seller. What the bank did was *monetize in advance* a commercial claim—to provide temporarily the money that was forthcoming anyway, and not much later either.

Note that the debtor had been credited with only 75 per cent of the sale's value; he, or someone for him, had to put up the rest. Someone had to risk $25,000 to make the transaction creditworthy. That alone limits the expansion of the money volume for such deals. And the number of such deals is limited for other reasons. The debtor himself must be creditworthy; often, shipping documents are required. The bank has to be convinced that a genuine, productive deal had been consummated, in which all concerned are beyond doubt, including the buyer on the other side or *his* banker who guarantees for him.

These *qualitative controls*, exercised by the prudent banker, mean an "invisible" *quantitative restraint* that is essential in maintaining a balance between the increase of loans (and deposits) and the growth of marketable output.

INFLATIONARY MONETIZATION

Now, suppose that the government borrows from the bank on a three-month treasury bill. Superficially, no difference exists between the two cases; in fact, the government's credit is better than the merchant's credit. Buying "short treasuries" is a very convenient transaction, involving no problem of qualitative control. It does not take an experienced, "prudent" banker to do this sort of business. But there is a world of monetary difference. The government is supposed to repay the short-term loan out of tax revenues. If it did, inflation would not occur any more than in the case of a commercial loan. Unfortunately, this is not the case. The government is in debt at the banks and may stay in debt (unless the public buys the short-term debt certificates from the banks, which it does for temporary holding only).

One-half the marketable national debt is bor-

THE "MODUS OPERANDI" OF INFLATION

rowed from the banking system, including the federal reserve banks. The latter's bond portfolio has increased almost 120-fold in less than thirty years and is now (September, 1960) much larger than the gold reserve: nearly $27 billion the one, under $19 billion the other. Contrary to the original statutes that restricted its operations mainly to the rediscounting of short-term commercial paper, the Federal Reserve System now carries virtually no commercial paper at all. The central bank, the last resort of the credit system, is in all but name a holding company for public securities.

By far the greater part (six-sevenths) of the mass of public debt owed to the banking system is of more than one-year maturity, not "short" even in name. Short or long, the bonds are being held by institutions which paid for them by creating spendable funds, with no counterpart in purchasable goods. The government acquires deposits, representing the monetization of sheer "paper," and uses them to pay its deficit. The purchasing power thus put in circulation stays there. It has to; it did not grow out of commercial transactions that would provide for the money's backflow. Nor has it a counterpart in tax revenues. Instead of liquidating its debt to the banks, the government keeps rolling it over and borrows additionally from time to time. And the money issued by the banks keeps turning around. Not one of every hundred dollars borrowed by the government—

whether it was used to stockpile unsalable farm products or to finance global give-away programs —has added anything to the nation's stock of productive, self-regenerating capital.

Small wonder that prices have doubled—more than doubled, on the average—since 1939. If they did not rise more, it is chiefly because of the great progress achieved by business in reducing costs by technological and organizational economies.

LIQUIDITY—BY INFLATION

As a matter of bookkeeping, the Federal Reserve System is a part of our banking system. In essence, it is much more than just another bank. It is the central organ of the entire credit structure. The fundamental import of its function may be shown by reverting to our earlier illustration, the New Orleans bank that loaned money on a cotton transaction.

On top of all the "inhibitions," or qualitative controls, that limit the individual bank's loaning propensity, there is one more that should be mentioned: the necessity for the banker to keep his house "liquid." This is his legal and moral duty, as one entrusted with the public's money. The deposits, even the savings, have to be paid out whenever the depositors draw checks or ask for cash. Obviously, if the bank is not to be closed, it must have enough cash resources available to fulfill such drains as may reasonably be expected.

THE "MODUS OPERANDI" OF INFLATION

The law requires that the member banks keep a fraction of their liabilities deposited at a federal reserve bank as a primary reserve. Sheer prudence requires that another fraction should be kept in the form of assets that can be turned quickly into cash. These "quick assets" are the banker's secondary line of defense. In our system, as it has operated since 1933, this secondary liquidity consists essentially of treasury obligations.

The point is that the credit expansion of commercial banks is limited by liquidity considerations. Since the law requires (on the average) 10 per cent of the bank's liabilities to be held in "cash," and prudence requires at least another 30 per cent to be readily available in the shape of "short treasuries," the bank's ability to create purchasing power is trimmed accordingly.

So far, so good. The rub is that these reserves are literally produced by the Federal Reserve System. It has the power to do so,[2] and it makes ample use of this power. That is the difference between the rank and file of banks on the one hand and the central bank on the other. Both create purchasing power, but the former would soon be stymied (except for gold inflow) if the latter did not provide the ultimate means of payment which keep the deposits convertible into cash and the banks from going broke. Thereby, the credit expansion, whether sound or not, is being kept going.

AN INFLATION PRIMER

THE CENTRAL ENGINE OF INFLATION

Technically, the Federal Reserve has three direct methods by which to provide the banks with "liquidity," enabling them to extend credit to the economy. It "rediscounts" (buys) such short-term commercial paper as the banks may offer, if they have any to offer. It makes "advances" to them, usually using government obligations as collateral. Or it buys federal securities, mostly of the short-term variety, in the open market, the proceeds being credited to the bank account of the dealer who sold the obligations. In any case, the banks acquire balances at a federal reserve bank and their worries over cash reserve requirements are over (for the time being).

In the process, the Reserve System accomplishes something else that goes far beyond its proper function and begets a nefarious inflationary drift. Indirectly, the Federal Reserve provides the member banks with their "secondary" reserves as well. It does so by creating a safe and secure market for public securities, U.S. Treasury bills, certificates, and notes, in particular. Within that one-year maturity range alone, there are some $70 billion available. (Another $115 billion in up to ten-year maturities are virtually supported, too.) Thereby, these securities become equivalent to cash. Their monetization by the banks and re-monetization by the Reserve System is the hard core of the process

THE "MODUS OPERANDI" OF INFLATION

by which the currency is being diluted—and the door opened for nefarious manipulations. Especially, the politicians' "freedom" to run the federal budget into deficits is greatly enhanced when nothing more serious seems to be at stake than throwing a few billions of additional "short treasuries" on the market.

1. "Banks" include commercial and mutual savings institutions as well as the Federal Reserve System. The savings and loan associations are savings banks, too, but in the statistics they do not appear among the banks.

2. The sole legal limitation of that power is a 25 per cent gold (certificate) reserve requirement against the Federal Reserve System's own notes and deposits. But at this writing, it still might go to the length of some $28 billion of new legal money before reaching that limit—which the Congress then might lower again, as it did in 1945.

III

THE FOUNTAINHEADS OF INFLATION

THE MONEY-PRINTING AUTOMAT

The Federal Reserve System is wrapped in forbidding technicalities and regulations. Yet the principles of its operation are so simple as to be within easy reach of the average person who wishes to understand them.

Neither the Federal Reserve System (and its organ, the Open Market Committee) nor the twelve reserve banks are banks in the common sense of the word, as mentioned before. Profit is not their objective; most of the money they earn goes to the Treasury. They take no deposits from an individual or an ordinary business firm, and give very few of them loans. Together, they constitute the central bank of the nation, dealing chiefly with the member banks; with the U.S. Treasury; with the governments or central banks of foreign countries, and, for the purchase and sale of federal obligations, with selected security dealers.

With this position as a central bank goes the monopoly of *issuing legal tender*—bank notes. The federal reserve banks have the privilege of making the money with which to pay for their own liabilities. The liabilities are created by the member bank borrowing on a treasury bill or similar security and drawing out a dollar note or a dollar balance, as it chooses. The note goes into circulation; the balance becomes the reserve on which the member bank "pyramids" its own deposit liabilities. (The nonmembers use as their reserves mostly balances held at member institutions.)

The process is further simplified if the Federal Reserve, instead of waiting for the member banks to ask for money, proceeds on its own by buying treasury paper on the open market in order to ease the money market and to lower the interest rates. Or conversely, it may sell treasury obligations to tighten the market and to "up" the rates.

All of which is as it should be. But the portfolio of the Reserve System is bulging with treasury securities in lieu of commercial paper. Treasury securities are the documentary evidence of federal deficits, past and present. Their bulk stems from the last war. The Treasury does not have to run fresh deficits every year (as it did in the fiscal year 1958–59 to the tune of a peacetime record $12.4 billion). Of its shortest term marketable debt, maturing within one year, $53 billion were at this writing in commercial banks, savings institutions, and other private portfolios. Theoretically, at least $53 billion worth of short paper *could* still be turned into legal tender! Nothing of the sort

AN INFLATION PRIMER

would be possible if the central bank would stick to its function, as was originally intended, and monetize only credit instruments which represent genuinely commercial, productive transactions of the self-liquidating type.

No inflation of runaway dimensions is to be expected (as yet); but the monetization of the public debt does not have to go anywhere near the theoretical limit in order to permit a fresh outbreak of price boosts. Assuming an average reserve ratio of one to six, the monetization of $1 billion permits an additional credit expansion of $6 billion, or so. And the flood can rise even without further debt monetization by the central bank, which has additional powers available to make or to break the inflation—by changing the member banks' reserve requirements.

MANAGED MONEY—THE ONE-WAY ROAD

The member banks, to repeat, must cover their

MEMBER BANK RESERVE REQUIREMENTS

	Percentage of Net Demand Deposits*			Percentage of Time (Savings) Deposits, All Member Banks
	Central reserve city banks†	Reserve city banks	Country banks	
Maximum	26	20	14	6
Minimum	13	10	7	3
Actual, Aug. 1, 1960	18.0	16.5	11	5

*Demand deposits *minus* cash items in process of collection and demand balances due from domestic banks.
†New York and Chicago.

THE FOUNTAINHEADS OF INFLATION

deposits by holding a fraction of them in balances at their respective reserve banks. But what fraction? This, the pertinent question, is answered in the accompanying table.

Note the broad range of discretionary power in the hands of the managers (who may be under the thumbs of the politicians). Within the broad legal limits, they can cut the reserve requirements or raise them. This is called an "elastic currency." In June, 1954, to overcome a mild recession (and to strengthen Mr. Eisenhower's chances come November), the Board of Governors lowered the banks' reserve requirements, boosting their lending capacity by a hefty $9 billion. This helped to bring about an unprecedented borrowing boom, but the bank reserves were not restored to their previous levels. The performance of the Board was repeated on the eve of the next presidential election: by September, 1960, the member banks' lending capacity was boosted by another $3.6 billion.

This sort of elasticity pervades the whole monetary system. Under the gold standard the minimum gold reserve against the central banks' liabilities was permanently fixed. It used to be mandatory for the Federal Reserve to hold gold equal to at least 40 per cent of its outstanding notes and 35 per cent of its deposit liabilities. The rule has been relaxed to permit an over-all 25 per cent minimum and could be relaxed further at the whim of Congress. The legal ceiling over the public debt was to be raised in a national emergency only. Since 1954 it has been raised four times in less than six years. No more monetary inhibitions! Floors may be lowered and ceilings raised on short notice.

The power of reducing the legal reserve requirements is dynamite, one would think. The Congress thinks otherwise. With the blessing of the Federal Reserve authorities, it has cut the requirements for the big banks in New York and Chicago to the level of the reserve city banks, as of 1962. Also, it permitted the banks to count the surplus cash in their tills as part of their legal reserves. This alone adds another 0.5 per cent to the big banks' potential and an estimated 3 per cent to that of the small ones. To clinch it all, the political heat is put on the Federal Reserve Board to abandon the "bills only" policy—it should buy long-term bonds as well! And the Treasury pleads for the right to sell more than the permissible $5 billion bonds direct to the central bank—to push them down its throat, as it were.

INFLATION BY "DEBT MANAGEMENT"

On paper, the Reserve System has virtually every power to maintain *monetary discipline* and to stem the inflation. It is under no legal obligation to grant credits to the member banks, still less to buy government bonds. It could skim off

THE FOUNTAINHEADS OF INFLATION

the liquidity of the money market and force interest rates upward. The mere refusal to grant credit to the banks in proportion to the expansion of their loans may spell the end of an ominous inflationary boom. The March, 1951, gentlemen's agreement between the Treasury and the Federal Reserve Board liberated the latter from the self-assumed war-time obligation to monetize the national debt, or to hold interest rates down. Ever since, our central bank has been pursuing, supposedly, a "flexible" policy: it commonly adjusts its discount rate—the fee it charges on its loans—to the market rather than forces a rate on the market. In principle, interest rates may rise or fall without interference. In actual practice, they are not permitted to rise, nor bond prices to fall, to a level that would curb the inflation for any appreciable length of time. The debt monetization continues, rain or shine, with interruptions few and far between.

The 1951 agreement between the Treasury and the Federal Reserve authorities would have made possible a truly "flexible" policy, had the former lived up to its implicit part of the deal. There should have been no more deficits in the budget; in any case, no major deficit. The Treasury should also have proceeded to convert a substantial slice of its short-term debt into longer maturities. It did nothing of the sort; instead, the volume of short maturities has been increasing practically year after year, despite the fact that there were ample occasions—recessions—when low interest rates obtained on the capital market and conversion operations would have been perfectly feasible.

There is the crux of the situation. Every stabilization attempt undertaken by the Federal Reserve authorities is, despite their good intentions, stymied from the outset. They are stymied for the simple reason that the Reserve System is "a creature of Congress" that can set down the law. In any case, the central bank cannot let the credit of the over-indebted national administration go to pot, which is what would happen if the "printing press" would cease to support a prodigal Treasury. This is called Treasury-Federal-Reserve-co-operation-in-managing-the-national-debt. What is being managed is a progressive inflation, imposed by the Congress. The heads of the Reserve System have no choice but to serve the fiscal interest, or resign. The latter they rarely do voluntarily. Instead, they rationalize the inflationary policies forced upon them into a policy of maintaining an "orderly market" for federal securities and guaranteeing general "stability." "Price stability, with full employment and continued growth" is the slogan to which the monetary authorities pay unrelenting lip service.

How that is accomplished is illustrated by a recent statement by Mr. William McChesney Martin, Jr., Chairman of the Board of Governors,

THE FOUNTAINHEADS OF INFLATION

before the Joint Economic Committee of Congress. He took pride in the many devices by which the national currency had been diluted in the first nine months after the onset of the 1957–58 recession:

From late Fall 1957 through April 1958, there were *four reductions in* Federal Reserve Bank *discount rates,* from 3½ per cent to 1¾ per cent. Through continuing open market operations from late Fall of 1957 to early last Summer, the Reserve System *supplied the* commercial *banks with some $2 billion of reserve funds.* Through *three successive reserve requirement reductions* in late Winter and early Spring of last year, the system released for the use of member banks about $1.5 billion of their required reserves.

The total amount of reserve funds supplied by the system to commercial banks over the nine months, November 1957–July 1958, was enough to enable member banks to reduce their discounts at the Reserve Banks from $800 million to about $100 million, to offset sales of gold to foreign countries amounting to about $1.5 billion, and to finance a commercial bank credit expansion of almost $8 billion. *Monetary expansion* from February through July *stimulated by* this *Federal Reserve action was* at an exceptionally rapid rate—*at an annual rate of 13 per cent* for all deposits. . . . (Italics supplied.)

The peacetime record 13 per cent annual rate of bank-deposit expansion coincided with a 16 per cent ($14 billion) deficit in the national budget. It was followed by a 12 per cent decline of our gold stock.

Since mid-1958, the Federal Reserve has taken some easy steps to drain the "water" from under the boom, raising security margin requirements

25

from 60 to 90 per cent, reducing somewhat the credit it extends, and upping the discount rate gradually to 4 per cent. But just previously, the volume of its outstanding credits—the monetary base on which the inflation is built—had been increased by $2.2 billion in 14 months. That helped to enlarge the money volume (cash in circulation and bank deposits) by $14 billion and to rekindle the inflationary boom.

By 1960, not only did the bill purchasing restart, but the discount rate was reduced again to 3 per cent, at a time when the European central banks were raising their rates. Also, the security margin requirements were lowered from 90 to 70 per cent and the reserve requirements of the (over-lent) member banks cut by $605 million,[1] as mentioned before.

The Federal Reserve System's freedom of action is limited for a further reason: it has to contend with the fact that the national government is a large-scale operator on the capital market. Its borrowing, debt rolling-over, and converting operations impede time and again the policy of the central bank. Moreover, the Administration is in the business of lending money and guaranteeing credits. In 1958, the total of loans extended and underwritten amounted to $43 billion. When one arm of the government tries to restrain reckless borrowing by raising the cost and the other arm promotes such borrowing by providing cheap

THE FOUNTAINHEADS OF INFLATION

funds, the result is irresponsibility and sheer confusion.

1. The loans-to-demand deposits ratio of the big New York banks stood in August, 1960, at 86 per cent, just four percentage points below the 1929 high!

IV

THE VICIOUS SPIRALS

THE PARABLE OF THE HORSE AND THE TROUGH

The Congress votes expenditures without revenues to cover them. The Administration finances the deficit by issuing IOU's that are the equivalent of cash. The banks convert many of them into active purchasing power and draw from the Federal Reserve System the cash balances for legal reserves. This house of paper rests on the central bank's readiness, voluntary or otherwise, to monetize the IOU's which represent no productive effort, no salable goods, no gold, not even tax revenues—in effect, nothing but promises, not to pay but to be renewed, with more of the same to come.

Come they do, be it out of the Treasury's fresh deficits and the exchange of new "shorts" (bills, certificates, and notes) for longer bonds, coming to maturity, or out of the accumulated portfolios of the public. In the ten months to the end of April, 1959, the bulky volume of outstanding marketable short-term treasury paper grew by no less than $23.6 billion, all but $0.2 billion available for monetization by the Reserve System.

A continued process of this sort is bound to bring about a trend of rising prices unless the excess money vanishes into hoarding (which it is not likely to do). Yet it was many years before the public showed signs of awakening to the inflation threat and to the role the money element plays in it. Even now, a variety of arguments is being offered to evade the money problem by blaming the rise of prices on symptoms of the inflation rather than on the underlying cause. Some economists still deny that rising prices have anything to do with the quantity of money thrown on the market. They argue that the funds accumulate in the banks, which do not rush to make loans just because they have the money on hand. There must be a legitimate demand growing out of real production to induce the banks to lend. It is one thing, they say, to lead the horse to water—quite another thing to make it drink.

One wonders whether the expert who argues this way has ever taken a horse to the trough. If he did, just how long did it take before the horse developed a "legitimate" thirst?

The parable does not do justice to the horse, which never drinks more water than it currently needs. But men plan by future prospects, real or imaginary. A heretofore submarginal demand for a bank loan becomes creditworthy when future earning prospects brighten—as they may in the light of a sustained flow of purchasing power in the channels of trade. It may take time, but an excessive money supply cannot fail to increase the demand for goods and services except in a depression, when it is used to liquidate an excessive volume of private debt.

COST-PUSH INFLATION?

When prices rise, few people take the trouble to look up the statistical data about debt monetization and bank-credit expansion. Still fewer seem to be aware of the causal relationships. What they do see is a sequence that has become virtually fixed: wages jump first, commodity prices limp behind them. Hourly wage rates fell slightly between 1929 and 1933, whereas the price level took a 40 per cent beating. But pretty soon both started to rise, wages leading the procession.

Then, during World War II, prices were "frozen" by controls, but pay rates could not be restrained. As the controls were scrapped toward the end of 1945, inflation took, within two years, a 30 per cent toll of the dollar's purchasing power in retail trade, paralleling simultaneous wage boosts. Ever since, price movements have lagged behind wage increases, as summarized in the following table.

Notice at once in the table that the data do not include fringe benefits paid by employers. These may amount to as much as 20 per cent of the wage bills, and they too keep mounting.

Of course, costs may have a decisive influence on prices, and labor is the number-one ingredient of costs. If labor's remuneration goes up faster than its productivity, prices tend to follow, calling in turn for compensation by higher wages, and a vicious cost-price spiral gets under way. But why do wages rise? There are two stock answers in (political) circulation. According to the one, presented largely by union spokesmen, labor merely claims its share in the rising profits which business

MAJOR PRICE MOVEMENTS AND FACTORY WAGES SINCE WORLD WAR II*
(Indexes: 1947–49 = 100)

	Consumer Prices	Wholesale Prices		Average Hourly Earnings (Mfg.)
		All commodities	Industrial commodities	
Postwar inflation				
January 1946.....	77.8	69.6	72.1	$1.003
January 1948.....	101.3	104.5	102.0	$1.302
Per cent change...	+30.2	+50.2	+41.5	+29.9
"Relative stability"				
January 1948.....	101.3	104.5	102.0	$1.302
June 1950........	101.8	100.2	102.2	$1.453
Per cent change...	+0.5	−4.1	+0.2	+11.6
Korean inflation				
June 1950........	101.8	100.2	102.2	$1.453
June 1951........	110.8	115.1	116.2	$1.599
Per cent change ..	+8.8	+14.9	+13.7	+10.0
"Relative stability"				
June 1951........	110.8	115.1	116.2	$1.59
June 1955........	114.4	110.3	115.6	$1.87
Per cent change...	+3.3	−4.2	−0.5	+17.6
Creeping price rises				
June 1955........	114.4	110.3	115.6	$1.87
June 1958........	123.7	119.1	125.3	$2.12
Per cent change...	+8.1	+8.0	+8.4	+13.4

*Source: U.S. Department of Commerce, Bureau of Labor Statistics.

draws by the upward "administration" of prices and by the ever rising "productivity" of the workers. According to another school of thought, the trade-unions enjoy monopoly power and use it ruthlessly. This supposedly causes the price inflation, which then provokes fresh credit demand, to be supported by debt monetization. We start on this second theory.

The large unions (and some of the small ones) do have a monopolistic position, though not because of the right to organize and to bargain on an industry-wide scale. Whether there is one union covering the entire steel industry or twenty-five organizations in as many districts or plants makes little difference in bargaining power. How can one forbid unions to co-operate, either in requesting identical pay boosts or in going on strike simultaneously? Where, indeed, should the geographic or professional lines be drawn to distinguish the monopolistic from the legitimate kind of union without being arbitrary and depriving the workers of their fundamental right to organize and to protect their legitimate interests?

Industrial conflicts are as old as the modern industrial system. Wages went up during booms before there was collective bargaining by unions. What has distinguished the American labor market since the New Deal legislation of the 1930's is the loss by the worker of his right to choose the men to represent him, or to bargain for himself. Once a union is recognized by the National Labor Board as the bargaining agency, the member is,

THE VICIOUS SPIRALS

in effect, coerced into accepting a leadership that may be in the hands of racketeers. In a majority of states even the "right to work" can be denied the employee who refuses to join a union and to pay dues. Hence, a monopolistic position is achieved, strengthened by resort to the intimidation of nonconforming members, use of strikebreakers, violence, and mass picketing, extortion from employers, unfair secondary boycotts, and corrupt and criminal practices. By their methods of restraining trade, the unions violate written and unwritten rules of the free market. Referring to two of the most powerful unions, a Senate committee's (minority) report stated in early 1960: "Corruption, misappropriation of funds, bribery, extortion and collusion with the underworld has existed in the U.A.W. as in the Teamsters. . . ." The unions, it seems, are above the law. And the law, or its administration, actually protects them.[1]

Yet the monopoly power of the unions is not the decisive force that drives labor costs in the stratospheric direction. Just how high could the *general* level of wages—not just in individual industries—go in the face of consumer resistance to higher prices, if people's pocketbooks were not replenished again and again by fresh money shots-in-the-arm? Patently, the magic circle of higher wages, higher prices, still higher wages, and so on, would break at the ultimate hurdle, the consumer's ability to pay. The trouble is that the total of in-

33

comes is being artificially maintained and expanded. If consumer incomes falter, the government steps in by disbursing funds or guarantees for public works, public housing, road building, farm subsidies, commodity stockpiling, foreign aid, mortgage credits, social security, and many other welfare objectives. The open and concealed subsidies, handouts, and "contracyclical" financial contraptions come out of the government's credit and the taxpayers' pockets, supplemented and supported by debt monetization, thus setting bank credit on the expansion road. That does it.

Rising labor costs are not the ultimate cause of the inflationary drift. They are a *prime transmission line* that connects the money inflation with the price inflation. The cause lies deeper, in the political arena where the unions' ultimate responsibility enters. The unions are the prime moving and lobbying force behind the official spending and money-manipulating policies which result in over-full employment and labor shortage. When the demand is strong and the supply short, the price tends to go up. That is what the nation's strongest pressure group puts over with an uncanny ability to sublimate its own *un*enlightened interest—the union officials', not the workers', interest—into national eminence. It uses ruthlessly the vote-commanding power of a superorganization, plus the influence provided by the multimillion dollars of members' dues at the bosses'

THE VICIOUS SPIRALS

free disposal. The worker's interest is lower product prices, steady employment at good pay, more savings to finance more work opportunities, all of which is negated in the long run by union policies.

To be sure, there are other pressure groups—groups of organized business and farm; veterans; bureaucrats; special interests in construction, mining, shipping, and shipbuilding; exporters, mortgage lenders, educationalists, and a host of other lobbies—that pull the inflationary strings for the benefit of their respective niches in the welfare state (while preaching the gospel of free enterprise). A "liberal" intelligentsia contributes its share in confounding a confused public. (Some *literati* still judge industrial capitalism in the light of the bygone sweatshops or of monopolies predating the Sherman and Clayton acts.) But organized labor delivers the strongest, most vocal, and most aggressive lobbying force on the inflationary side.

BUILT-IN INFLATION

Inflation is being brought about by the combined efforts of pressure groups in and out of the Congress. Such groups are largely responsible for current budget deficits as well as for inducing the central bank to monetize debt and to sustain an excessive flow of purchasing power—at a cumulative rate averaging 6 per cent or more, double or treble the rate at which the *real* output of the nation is growing.

Unions or no unions, boom or recession, wage costs are bound to rise when the growing money supply appears on the market place as an artificially boosted demand for labor's services. Employers' resistance to union claims is stymied in an economic climate saturated with the expectation that the money tokens are readily forthcoming—if the consumer will not pay, the government will. Higher pay (often for less work) and more fringe benefits in one industry with rising labor productivity spreads to others in which no progress in efficiency obtains. And every rise in costs that helps to force prices upward becomes embedded in the price structure by way of contractural *escalators*, automatically adjusting wage rates to each fractional increase of the cost-of-living index. Nor is that the only vicious circle set in motion by the ceaseless or recurrent process of debt monetization.

A most significant effect of the wage-price inflation is the *temporary incentive for new (mal-) investments in plant and equipment*. Business is "pushed" into labor-saving devices in order to economize on labor costs, and it is being "pulled" into false capacity expansion by the growing demand for products, a consequence of higher money incomes and of a deceptive prosperity. As prices climb and the inflationary mentality spreads, a further motive becomes operative: the urge to hedge on the inflation. The cumulative effect would be a runaway inflation, if the process were not interrupted every third year or so by a recession, with each interruption sharper and more painful than the last. An overheated economy burns its bearings, as it were, by running up against labor and capital shortages and losing its flexibility, while overexpansion boomerangs in declining profits.

With jerks and screeches, inflation progresses. Under the cloak of immunity from the penal code, from the laws of corporation and monopoly regulation, even from the Constitution's provision for the individual's liberty to join or not to join private organizations, the unions proceed to drive the economy toward inflation. But there is a price to be paid. In the jingle of K. E. Boulding (1951):

> We all, or nearly all, consent
> If wages rise by ten per cent
> It puts a choice before the nation
> Of unemployment or inflation.

The choice is not between depression and inflation, as the advocates of 2–5 per cent annual price increases pretend. The choice is between monetary stability on the one hand, and inflation with recurrent mass unemployment on the other.

The fiscal and monetary "stabilizers" prescribed by the (unwritten) code of inflation are in full operation. But the law of supply and demand asserts itself: 5 per cent of the (overpaid) labor force stays unemployed in the midst of super-booms, "liberal" credits, and $135 billion total public expenditures a year.

1. The 1959 labor legislation somewhat moderates unions' power, though not essentially. The unions remain in control of the labor supply, under the cloak of the union shop, and they are practically exempted from prosecution even for criminal action. They still can control labor efficiency under the protection of "work rules," grievance procedures, etc. State and local authorities, often even the courts, favor unsavory union practices.

V
RIDING ON THE INFLATION CREST

SPREADING THE INFLATION

Inflation is a monetary phenomenon pure and simple. There is no such thing as an inflation by "wage-push," or by "profit-push." Both are consequences, not ultimate causes. It is not rocking the boat that makes the storm, but the rocking helps to sink the boat.

The cause is the excessive volume of credit, sparked by the debt-monetization practices of the central bank under the self-assumed function, since 1938, of "maintaining an orderly market" for government securities. No such function was originally intended or written into the statutes of the Federal Reserve System. It is a pretext and fancy name to cover up the reality, which is to permit Washington to indulge in fiscal irresponsibility.

To eliminate the last shred of doubt about the ultimate and effective cause of inflation, consider the following. In April, 1959, the union of 1,250,000 steel workers put up extravagant claims, estimated as a billion dollar "package." Marriner S. Eccles, former chairman of the Federal Reserve

Board (and a one-time rabid New Dealer) commented: "If all of the other workers of America—more than 65 million—were to demand and receive these same benefits, it would add 52 billion dollars to the cost of goods produced. There would be nothing 'creeping' about the resulting inflation." And that would not be the end of it; rising prices would call for further wage-cost increases, and so on.

The point is that an important wage boost tends to give the entire wage structure an upward impetus, and, unless the additional costs are somehow offset, the price level will tend to rise, too.[1] But where would a majority of entrepreneurs find the cash with which to pay? They could scarcely have the money tucked away to add 10 per cent or more to their labor costs. Nor would the consumers want to deplete their savings or default on their taxes and debts. The enhanced wages could not be paid unless the banks came to the rescue of the public and the central bank to the rescue of the banks. Short of a substantial shot-in-the-arm, markets and prices would break and massive unemployment develop. The history of inflation offers innumerable cases which show that the most elaborate and automatic spirals cease to operate as soon as the credit flow to feed them stops.

The cost-push theory of inflation assumes that costs are the sole, or main, determining factor of prices, as if demand had nothing to do with it.

What about subsidized prices? Surely the unions are not to be blamed for the fact that in the country with the world's greatest surplus of farm output—and with official farm stockpiles worth some $10 billion—basic farm-commodity prices are up to 50 per cent higher than they are on the world markets.

THE FALLACY OF BUILT-IN STABILIZERS

The money-printing press is the source of the wage-push and of all other inflationary phenomena, including the fake devices to protect the economy against a depression.

Social Security benefits, guaranteed annual wages, long-term wage agreements, cartelized (minimum) prices, redeemable savings bonds, and so on, have been presented to the public as built-in stabilizers to provide cushions against a depression. They provide nothing of the sort. They are just some of many pretexts for inflating the currency. For example, the reserves of the Social Security program, built up by contributions of the "insured," consist of government bonds that would have to be sold—to the banks, presumably. Guaranteed wages guarantee nothing; they merely imply that there will be sufficient cash flow forthcoming to sustain them.

There are, indeed, stabilizers that can stop the inflation. They are not built in by law or by policy; they are part and parcel of the free market's automatism, and they are very effective, as shown by the recurrence of recessions which interrupt the spiraling process of inflation. However, as soon as the cycle goes in reverse, a money outpour is let loose and the genuine stabilizers are swept away.

THE PRODUCTIVITY DEBATE

Coming back to the spiral: time and again the unions claim that their wage demands need not affect costs. All they are asking for is more money for more output, supported by statistics to show the rising "productivity" of labor. For good measure, the claim was confirmed by no less an authority than General Motors Corporation. The great automobile maker beat the gun by offering in 1952 an annual productivity wage escalator—a memorable case for big business co-operating with a big union at the expense of the public.

There was a byplay, too. GM agreed to the (compulsory!) union shop, selling its employees' freedom of choice down the union river.

Output per man-hour or man-day has risen and keeps rising in many branches of manufacturing. But the productivity argument is a rationalization to surround labor's inflation-borne power of coercion with a halo of economic (and ethical?) sanctity. The trouble is, in the first place, that wages rise in all industries, whether or not there is an improvement in efficiency. Barbers, beauticians, florists, repair men, house painters, and morticians get wage boosts with no perceptible increase of output per man-hour. In fact, "services" take a growing share in total employment and lead in the successive increases of the cost of living.[2]

What is meant by labor productivity? The number of physical units produced per man-day or man-shift is a convenient statistical device to measure efficiency, but it has no more to say about labor's contribution to the productive process than has the ratio of energy units used (or of dollars of capital applied) to the volume of output. If it takes but one man to do the job of two, it is most likely because of technological or organizational progress brought about by fresh capital investment, new inventions, managerial skill, or better utilization of resources rather than by any effort of the workers who attempt to reap the benefits.

The very concept of labor productivity is open to question. In a plant, is it the average output of all workers or of the actual machine operators only that matters? For an industry as a whole, what does average productivity mean in the face of vast differences among individual plants? Over a period of time, ratios between labor input and product output become irrelevant if qualitative product improvements occur or if the product changes altogether. Is physical productivity significant, or productivity in terms of dollars? The pitfalls are legion. Exact measurement is impossible.

LABOR DISINCENTIVES BY INFLATION

The spurious remuneration of labor's "productivity" is worlds apart from true incentive wages. By the latter, the enterpreneur pays for more or better work accomplishment. By the former, he buys peace for a while, often paying more money for less work. In the one case, there is a distinct relationship between work done and and payment received. In the other case, labor is frequently paid for someone else's accomplishment. In the workers' eyes, the credit for their raise in income goes to the bargaining, if not extorting, union that exploits the inflation-swelled demand for the products, and little or no credit is given to the capitalist, manager, salesman, or engineer who may be truly responsible for the enhanced productivity.

The outcome does not even provide durable peace between management and labor. Suffice it to mention that, between 1956 and 1958, wages in the basic steel industry went up 19 per cent while output per man-hour declined 7½ per cent; by mid-1959, the industry was hit by a nation-wide strike, the seventh in fourteen years.

More is at stake than wage rates, more also than fringe benefits. (The latter rise at times faster than do even the wage bills.) More is at stake than disputes and strikes. If costs per unit of output mount despite huge capital investments in ever more productive equipment, it is because of a further reason: the union-sponsored restrictive practices. Featherbedding, make-work, and similar devices, reminiscent of the medieval guild system, reach extraordinary intensity under creeping inflation, spreading cost increases throughout the economy. They amount to providing—on the railroads, especially—permanent jobs at full pay to men who work productively only part of the time or not at all. These practices (legalized by the courts!) frustrate technological progress, the ultimate source of higher wages and lower prices! Time and again, this erosion of productivity is accompanied by slowed-down labor effort, a high level of labor absenteeism, and an excessive rate of labor turnover, all typical by-products of over-full employment.

PRODUCTIVITY AND CAPACITY TO PAY

Wage boosts bear a very tenuous relationship, if any, to productivity. For the period from 1939

	%Increase in Average per Man-Hour Productivity	%Increase in Hourly Earnings without Fringe Benefits	%Increase in Hourly Earnings plus Fringe Benefits
Basic steel industry......	64	201	211
Railroads.......	86	185.6	190
All manufacturing industries..	48.8	214	*

*Complete data not available. In 1956, total fringe benefits paid by employers amounted to $12.2 billion.

to 1956, the following figures of the Bureau of Labor Statistics speak clearly.

The union bosses are never at a loss for an answer. Look at real wages—money wages corrected for changes in the dollar purchasing power—they say, and you will find that labor productivity outpaced them. The fact is that when hourly pay rises at the annual rate of about 5.3 per cent and per man-hour productivity increases by 2.3 per cent, the result is a 2.9 per cent net annual increase of unit labor costs. That is what happened to American manufacturing over a sixteen-year period. This is called wage inflation; it ought to be called: inflation carried on the "wings" of the unions. The unions not only generate the inflation through political action, but they also carry the virus and accelerate its spread. Since the 1930's generating, carrying, and accelerating the inflation seem to be their outstanding functions in the whole industrial world. The technique is the same almost everywhere: the use of their inflation-borne, unchecked power to extort monopolistic results.

If labor's "productivity" does not justify claims for higher wages and fringe benefits, then the increased cost of living will do—increased since the last wage blowup that preceded the price rises. If that argument is too transparent, the unions still may fall back on "ability to pay," which means, in essence, that you have to pay me simply because you have, or are supposed to have, enough money to give me what I want. What if profits decline? Why, of course, my wages have to be raised in any case. Heads I win, tails you lose.

1. Actually, wages do not rise in a uniform fashion, nor do prices. "Those who can raise prices most readily, or increase wages most effectively, or escalate themselves to a position of neutrality, get more and more of total income, while the unsheltered get less."—Federal Reserve Bank of New York, *Monthly Review*, June, 1959.

2. Between 1949 and June, 1958, the average "retail" price increase was 35.4 per cent for services and 15.9 per cent for merchandise.

VI
THE CONSUMER (AND TAXPAYER) BE DAMNED

WHO PAYS THE BILL?

Who carries the cost of inflated wages and fringe benefits, of shorter hours, of two men doing one man's job, and so on? There are several possibilities. The added cost may be offset by technological progress and labor-saving devices; it may be shifted on the consumer by higher prices or lower quality of goods, or on the taxpayer if the government steps in with subsidies; or it may come out of profits.

Inordinately rising unit labor costs cannot be offset indefinitely by economies in production and distribution. Some unions resist stricter work rules and new equipment. Labor-saving devices may not be available or may be too expensive, and the financing difficult. The incentive for their installation is lacking if the management realizes that any economies achieved are bound to call for fresh wage requests. The result may be fewer jobs and/or more intensive work requirements. Sooner or later, labor "pays" by what is called *technological unemployment:* higher wages for fewer workers.

If prices are raised, the cost of higher wages falls ultimately on the consumer. That includes the workers and their families, of course. As the price inflation spreads, their dollar gains tend to evaporate. It may take some time when the inflation is the creeping kind. When it accelerates, the gain rapidly turns, by all historic evidence, into a loss of real income. It should be remembered, incidentally, that the process of inflating incomes is in itself expensive. Except in revolutionary situations, no country has ever lost as many labor-days, either absolutely or percentagewise, due to strikes as has the United States in this post-World War II era. Strikes mean lost wages; the losses the employer suffers mean less demand for capital goods and less employment; shortages caused by strikes raise the cost of living; and the unions take a share of the worker's pocketbook, if not of his freedom.

Suppose the demand for the product is *elastic*, that is the consumer refuses to pay the higher price and the market shrinks. Anthracite is a textbook example; by extorting ever more wage dollars, Mr. John L. Lewis raised the unit costs so high that the consumer turned to substitute fuels. The industry is dying slowly but surely, and so are the jobs. Again, labor as a whole sooner or later pays the bill, partially or fully, for the wage increases.

The employer may recoup the increased labor costs by drawing public subsidies. In that case, taxes rise. And who pays those, if not the people engaged in production? There is one way, to the trade union way of thinking, to get "something for nothing": by taking the pay raise out of profits. That is the laborite (and self-styled liberal) battle-cry: Let the capitalist pay. All arguments of the unions converge, openly or by innuendo and insinuation, on the contention that as a matter of equity the "high" profits should be trimmed in favor of the workers. The idea seems to be always present in the back of certain minds that wages could be substantially higher, and without inflationary repercussions, if profits were lower— monopoly profits, in particular.

THE POT CALLS THE KETTLE BLACK

"Monopoly" is a nasty word. It connotes supply restriction in order to exploit the buyer. Under the Sherman and Clayton acts it has a legal, or rather illegal, status. The Department of Justice seems to be anxious to prosecute every case, real or alleged. (To do so is "good politics.") No one but an outright Communist charges American business in general with illegal conspiracy. However, economists have invented two novel terms which carry by innuendo the same connotation. Big Business is supposed to enjoy "oligopoly"— quasi-monopoly exercised by the few—or to "administer prices." Bigness somehow enables the largest firms of each industry to co-operate in controlling the respective markets. Proof is, supposedly, that (1) in industries such as steel, auto-

THE CONSUMER (AND TAXPAYER) BE DAMNED

mobiles, tobacco, and aluminum, two to four of the largest corporations control 50 per cent and more of the output; (2) they sell their wares at virtually identically fixed prices, following the "leader"; (3) prices are being "listed" or announced by the big suppliers.

In reality, there are no ingrained oligopolies or administered prices on the American scene, except where the government promotes them. The truth is that bigness per se provides no power in the price-making process; sharpest competition prevails among "leaders." The truth is that without governmental protection scarcely any industrial monopoly could carry on clandestinely in the face of prosecution, consumer resistance, and competition by substitutes. In fact, it is the government that limits competition and fosters monopolies by high tariffs, price supports, stockpiling, military procurement, subsidized housing, and many other policies.[1]

The truth is, also, that "administered" list prices may represent either the outcome of competition or mere balloons to test the market forces.[2] The truth is, finally—and this is economics on the (much neglected) undergraduate level—that *price uniformity is an essential characteristic of the competitive market.* Under free competition the price is set by the cheapest producer whose output is large enough to affect the supply; the others must follow the "leader," or lose out.

AN INFLATION PRIMER

Monopoly power is the ability of the supplier to exact a price higher than that prevailing under competitive conditions. There is such power in operation, not subject to the antitrust laws and exempt from the provisions of the criminal codes as well. The big unions have it—often the small ones, too. They enjoy a monopoly power of a width, breadth, and intensity the like of which never before existed in the United States. They use it ruthlessly, without any concern about the consumer or even about the future employment of their own members.

PROFIT INFLATION

Wage increases need not raise prices, union spokesmen say, if profits were not excessive. What makes for "high" (pre-tax) profits, one may ask? The answer is, ironically, that the unions themselves are largely responsible.

Time and again, the unions come out for public spending projects. They are most determined advocates of public housing and of credit (FHA) guarantees for private-dwelling construction. Their political influence, in alliance with the "construction lobby" of the business interests involved, goes a long way toward putting over what they advocate. This gives a great boost to the building industry—and more profits to the firms engaged in it.

This is one example of many. The unions are

THE CONSUMER (AND TAXPAYER) BE DAMNED

most vocal supporters of almost any special (profit) interest that can be promoted at the expense of the consumer or the taxpayer.

Some union leaders outdo the exporter, whose pocketbook is directly affected, in enthusiasm for our interminable foreign-aid program. They are motivated, or so they claim, by humanitarian sentiment for their fellow man. But no bleeding hearts inhibit their simultaneous lobbying for higher tariffs and quotas, which hurt that same foreigner's exports, in order to secure employment at higher wages for the union members—and more profits for the employers.

One would expect organized labor to object to farm subsidies which are a real burden on both the living costs and the tax bills of the urban masses. (The number of organized farm hands is too small to be of any weight.) Futile expectation! Greedy pressure groups may fight each other; they are brothers under the political skin when it comes to the common enemy, the general public.

There has been much comment on the lack of employer resistance against demands for wage raises. To a large extent, political pressures have been to blame. But often, much too often, a cynical sort of co-operation prevailed in labor-management disputes. A standard bargaining argument is: Why do you, the employer, object to raising wages when 52 per cent of the added cost is deductible from the corporate income tax and the remaining 48 per cent is easily shifted on the consumer's income? Let someone else worry about the fact that the Treasury's revenues may decline and its expenditures increase.

Above all, by promoting price inflation, the unions promote the dollar volume of sales; if the profit *margin* per unit of turnover remains the same, or does not fall too much, the gross return of business—in dollars of declining purchasing power—cannot go but upward. Actually, margins did drop in the last decade, but not enough to offset the effect of a growing volume of dollar sales. In any case, it is the *inflation of the money supply* that, by distending the demand for consumer and producer goods, *creates the sellers' markets* on which rising costs can be unloaded and profits maintained, or even increased. A sellers' market is a short way of saying that "too much money chases too few goods."

In the course of a price inflation, situations are bound to arise in which groups of entrepreneurs and speculators reap extraordinary windfalls. Yet, considering the decline of the money's purchasing power and the progressive rate of personal income taxation, the average *real* return on shares of stocks lags far behind *real* remuneration for the average labor-hour.[3] At that, a large sector of business itself does not even lay away enough reserves to provide for staying in business, still less to expand it. Insufficient reserves for the replacement of plant and equipment (at inflated prices!) and for future capital needs is a devastating effect of the prolonged currency dilution. In other words, we consume a large fraction of the capital required to provide a rapidly growing population with the tools and facilities for its livelihood. (The cost is $20,900 per worker in the country's largest corporations, according to an analysis of balance sheets by the First National City Bank, New York.)

Extraordinary (pre-tax) profits of the riskless kind, (lower-taxed) capital gains in particular, are sparked by the inflation. Capital gains remain largely on paper until either the estate levies or a depression wipes them out. Government orders on a cost-plus base often are another rich source of rewards for no-risk-taking, in violation of the free market's prime distributive rule. The consequent deterioration of business standards is a major contributory factor to the degeneration of union practices. If profits can be earned without incurring risk, why not wages without doing work?

1. This has been well brought out by Walter Adams and Horace M. Gray in *Monopoly in America* (New York: The Macmillan Company, 1955).

2. Allegedly administered prices may be just as flexible, up and down, as others. "The price on steel bars got changed as frequently as those on men's suits, wrist watches, and baseball gloves," reported the First National City Bank, New York (May, 1959).

3. From 1948 to the end of 1958, wages and salaries (including fringe benefits) paid by corporations increased from $90 billion to $158 billion. Corporate (after-tax) profits decreased from $20 billion to $18 billion a year.

VII

THE "PHILOSOPHY" OF INFLATION

OPPORTUNISM VERSUS PRINCIPLES

The sophisticated reader, if he has followed us so far, may raise a quizzical question. Our reasoning was based on an unproved thesis, he may say. It was taken for granted that monetary stability is a categorical imperative of policy. But we have seen axioms fade out even in geometry. In the age of relativity and four-dimensional space, doubt has evicted dogma, probability has replaced causality. (Did opportunism oust principle?) On what relevant grounds, other than an "antiquated" tradition, do we condemn the apparent historical trend accepted by a majority of progressive nations?

If ethics is a mere matter of anthropology or psychoanalysis, who is to proclaim immutable laws of economics? Must we revert to the laissez faire ("leave us alone") doctrine that is as obsolete—the self-styled modernist may continue—as are the gold standard and the "anarchistic" competition of the nineteenth century? (To collectivists, competition is always anarchistic or monopolistic.) In the collectivist gibberish: A dynamic world will not submit to a rule that has inhibited man-

THE "PHILOSOPHY" OF INFLATION

kind from seeking to "maximize the welfare of the many rather than the profits of the few." The gold standard in particular is the object of resentment and ridicule because of its "discipline"—the limit it sets on tinkering with the currency and arbitrarily manipulating the credit volume.

As a matter of fact, the apology for inflation is not so new or so undogmatic as it pretends to be. Nor is it generally accepted in some backward countries. Also, the alleged historical law of perpetual inflation is subject to change on short notice.[1] So is the inflationary philosophy itself, despite its scientific pretensions.

Indeed, the fashionable (statist and inflationary) economics is a reversion to the pre-nineteenth-century vintage, only more dogmatic and far more emotion loaded. A favorite device is to ridicule the opponents of inflation by charging them with being laissez faire believers. This implies, very explicitly, that the only alternative to permanent or recurrent inflation is to stop economic growth, accept massive unemployment, and let the unemployed starve on the streets. If we do not keep inflating, cost what it may, we shall lose the cold war or go bolshevist is the proverbial last word of the dyed-in-the-wool inflationist.

"MIND YOUR OWN BUSINESS"

In historical perspective, *laissez faire* was a reaction to centuries-long bureaucratic meddling, to the multitude of oppressive laws and regulations, and to the crushing monopolies of guilds and other privileged groups. All of this was enforced or at least tolerated by the state. Hence, the reaction: "Mr. Government, mind your own business." But what *is* the government's business in relation to the economy and, especially, to money?

None whatsoever—beyond defense and internal order—is the literal interpretation of economic freedom. Such is *not* our concept of freedom. We would not let the unemployed starve even if "economic rationality" would require it, which it does not. It is rational to *permit* wage rates to fall in order to overcome a depression by adjusting costs to declining prices; starving the unemployed in the intervening period, which may last many months, is quite another thing. Few of us would agree that the labor of children in early British factories and of women in the mines was justified because it speeded up capital accumulation out of high profits, or that "interventions" such as the eight-hour day, free grammar schools, and the graduated income tax smack of bolshevism. Nor is the rule of the free market an obstacle to welfare spending by the authorities—the local ones, preferably—provided the spending does not impair competition, financial stability, or the incentives to work, is not a pretext for servicing pressure groups, and is not fraught with corruption.

A prime misunderstanding should be cleared

THE "PHILOSOPHY" OF INFLATION

up at once. We must distinguish the institutional *guidance* of the economic process from its collectivist *control*. Objecting to the normal function of a central bank, which is to check an excessive flow of bank credit (illiquidity!), is typical of the pedants' confusion. By the same token, control of the traffic by a policeman might be objected to as an abridgment of human rights. Restraining monopolists is another interference with "freedom" that in reality preserves freedom.

The naive leave-us-alone idea enjoyed a measure of popularity in the nineteenth century and gave the period an undeserved black eye. Attempts in France and Britain to suppress the labor unions were instrumental in begetting the socialist movement. The theory of Marx that capitalism destroys itself was based on the totally false assumption, spread by the same laissez faire school, that labor as a group has virtually no chance of improving its lot. Capitalism might have destroyed itself had not worldly wisdom prevailed over the dogmatic misinterpretation of the perfectly sound doctrine: that the price mechanism of the free market brings about the most productive allocation of resources, the lowest possible prices, remuneration according to services rendered, and optimal (best) satisfaction of the consumer at his free choice. A by-product of free competition is low profit margins. Inflation, "the most deadly of all economic diseases," is a royal road to the burial of these functions and ultimately of economic freedom itself.

Unfortunately, the laissez faire (Manchester) school still has respectable adherents. The disservice these persons unwittingly render to the cause of free enterprise and sound money is a serious one. The more so, since the zealots of an obsolete Utopia outdo in their zeal the original. This is especially true in matters pertaining to monetary policy.

The "classical" protagonist of undiluted economic freedom considered the permanently *fixed price of gold* as a number-one pillar and an irrevocable condition of the free market. Some of his promient (self-appointed) successors would extend "freedom" to the price of the monetary unit itself. The gold value of the dollar, they argue, should fluctuate until it finds its "natural level." Why not let the length of the yard and the weight of the ton vary too? There is probably no more effective tool with which to inflate the monetary base on which the credit structure rests than tinkering with the currency's gold content. The same holds for a once-and-forever devaluation of the dollar, even if its propagandists, the special interests in gold mining, pretend that this is the royal road to "stabilization."

PERPETUAL PROSPERITY WITHOUT TEARS

It is deliberately misleading to pin the label

THE "PHILOSOPHY" OF INFLATION

laissez faire on the opponents of inflation; it is just as unfair to call every vindicator of inflation a communist, though inflation is a "bloodless" technique to revolutionize the economic system. The American devotee of progressive debt monetization may be sincere in wishing to rescue us from allegedly imminent depression. As a rule, he denies outright that he advocates rising prices and pooh-poohs the danger. Nay, he claims to be against both, inflation and "deflation"; he is for full employment, continued growth, and stable prices—by promoting inordinately rising wages, artificially low interest rates, and deficit spending.

The money-counterfeiting propensity takes innumerable forms. Economic incantations may cover up the orators' objectives. Here is a sample of oratory, delivered by Senator Paul H. Douglas, leader of the pour-out-cheap-money wing of the 86th Congress (he was on the opposite side eight years earlier):

"I believe that the American people desire that our economy meet three tests: providing maximum employment, an adequate rate of growth, and maintaining relative price stability and preventing both inflation and deflation."—*Congressional Record,* March 23, 1959, p. 4357.

Note the vagueness of the terms "maximum," "adequate," and "relative." The London *Economist*, by no means a believer in *laissez faire*, commented (August 29, 1959) in a typical English understatement: "Senator Douglas was once a prominent economist, but the life of politics has dulled his objectivity and diverted his attention."

The object of inflationist wishful thinking is the centuries-old dream of perpetual prosperity at no social cost. Money-printing does the trick. But even dreams have their fashions. At one time, minting silver was to deliver mankind, meaning the indebted farmer, from "crucifixion on a cross of gold." The 1920's developed a refined technique to keep rolling a reckless speculative mania, the "eternal prosperity on a high plateau": continuous credit expansion, in complete disregard of liquidity requirements.

Since the 1930's the "new economics" of the brilliant but whimsical J. M. Keynes has dominated the political scene and much of the academic teaching. One of his specious ideas was to monetize (inflate) in the depression and pump the money out (deflate) when full employment had been established. The underlying assumptions were two: that labor will not ask for higher wages even if prices rose (the unions are not interested in the cost of living, Keynes asserted), and that the inflationary process can be thrown in reverse gear whenever the money managers decide to do so (as if they were not only immaculately wise, but also omnipotent). But it is not possible, least of all in a relatively free economy, to create artificial employment by money administrations and not cause wage and price rises (in some sectors); and it is

THE "PHILOSOPHY" OF INFLATION

most impolitic even to attempt to break a prosperity wave by deflating the money volume.

Actually, although the depression faded out twenty years ago, we are still inflating. The definitions of full employment and of unemployment are adjusted conveniently to the "needs" of the pressure groups or are replaced by some arbitrary rate of growth, measured by a fictitious statistical standard. The authorities all along the Potomac have joined the courthouse politicians in solemn assertions that they can and will pursue the mutually exclusive objectives of inflation-fed full employment and maximum production, with guaranteed price stability thrown into the bargain, thus talking from both sides of their mouths, like Arthur T. Hadley's Microwac, the electronic robot running for the presidency.

THE RATIONALE OF THE CYCLE

Monetary "reformers" of every denomination were fishing in the troubled waters of the Great Depression, and they are still at it. Whatever economic creed they profess, all assume allegedly incurable shortcomings of "capitalism." It is supposed to be hopelessly exposed to recurrent mass unemployment, if not to perpetual stagnation. For one spurious reason or another, the markets are (supposedly) incapable of restoring their own equilibrium or even of maintaining it. This is the fundamental concept of Marxism as well as of

AN INFLATION PRIMER

Keynesianism. From there follows the call to collectivize the whole economy or at least the money and credit system. The difference is in degree rather than in substance. The radical departure and the so-called middle-of-the-road approach have in common the underlying economic philosophy: to substitute political fiat for the free functioning of markets and prices.

The crucial question then is: Why does every boom bust? The answer of the inflationist is simple and easy. Prosperity comes to a halt when money is scarce and credit dear. Accordingly, ample and cheaper money is the cure. The additional funds, the unions claim, should preferably go into higher wages to be spent by the masses, not to be hoarded or used for conspicuous consumption as the "capitalists" (allegedly) would do.

But what causes the "money shortage"? It denotes a *disequilibrium* between supply and demand. Creditors and debtors are overextended. The merchants may have overstocked, expecting higher prices and/or more sales. If they are disappointed, must they be supported by credit shots-in-the-arm? (Why not borrow the parity-price concept of our bankrupt farm policy by setting up an "ever-normal" general store and donate the surpluses to the backward countries? Moscow could never match *that*.) Inventory recessions are the necessary corrections of inventory booms. The latter would scarcely amount to much if the banks

THE "PHILOSOPHY" OF INFLATION

used proper caution in financing the accumulation of goods on the shelves. Relaxing credit after the goods become unsalable would be a clear invitation to the merchants to indulge in more of the same speculative stockpiling.

What justification is there for profits if the losses are to be nationalized? Capitalism has no economic or moral *rationale* if it is not what it should be: a system of risk-bearing, *profit*-earning and *loss*-taking enterprises. Indeed, profits (beyond managerial pay and interest on capital) are the remuneration for incurring the risk of losses.

Or, consider the investment cycles. When steel mills operate well below capacity or when newly built homes find no buyers, one or both of the following events have occurred. Steel capacity had been expanded too far and the final product is overpriced; too many houses were built at too high cost. Under stable monetary conditions, the natural correction will set in; prices (and costs) will fall until they meet the consumer demand, and business recovery ensues. Not so, if inflationary stimuli are applied. Construction may continue, customers or no customers. The "recession" is overcome, but costs and prices spiral and the excessive supply grows further, heading for a *real slump*.

PROGRESS OR "GROWTH"?

The downward swings of the (short) *inventory*

cycle and especially of the (much longer) *investment cycle* fulfill highly significant functions, best described as of sobering up effect. Parasitic firms that mushroom on the inflationary swing are eliminated. Bank liquidity is improved. Overexpension of plants and inventories is checked. Interest rates on fixed-value claims decline; the overvaluation of shares gives way to a recovery of the bond market. Speculative ventures are trimmed; rational investment standards come into their right. Labor and managerial efficiency improve dramatically, with or without new equipment. Costs per unit of output decline even *without wage rate cuts*. But, more often than not, high salaries *are* cut. Commodity prices, which have gone up on the expectation of continued inflation, soften, as do the unions' wage raise demands.

For illustration, a few headlines chosen at random from recent and very mild recessions will do: "Businessmen bank on permanent gains from emergency cost cuts" (September 1958). "Fear of unemployment brings drop in loafing, job-hopping, tardiness. Coffee breaks are shorter; work quality improves" (January, 1958). "Worker output on the increase as joblessness grows, firms push to cut costs . . . 20% gain in efficiency follows layoff. Absenteeism, 'quits' drop" (July, 1949).

"Fighting slump by cutting costs," headlined the *New York Times* in February, 1958; and the *Wall Street Journal:* "Companies save where they

THE "PHILOSOPHY" OF INFLATION

can during the business decline." While profits flow without much strain, it is only natural to neglect economies, to take it easy, to enjoy life and let the expense accounts run amok. When business turns down, output per worker that was sagging during the boom turns upward. Product quality and "service" to the customer improve spectacularly. These effects are by no means a matter of labor efforts alone. Of prime importance is enhanced managerial efficiency. The pressure of competitive imports spurred the textile mills' cost-cutting efforts: "On modest equipment spending they've achieved sharp improvements in productivity" (*Wall Street Journal,* May, 1960).

In fact, widespread misapprehensions notwithstanding, depressions are times of accelerated progress. As F. C. Mills, an outstanding statistician, has pointed out, the average *increase of* per-man *productivity* in American industry (ratio of physical output to man-hour input) was 2 per cent annually over the first half of this century; but two depression periods of an accelerated increase stood out—1918–24 and 1932–41.[2] Actually, during the Great Depression between 1933 and 1935, manufacturing output per man-hour rose 11 per cent, in spite of much product quality improvement, the U.S. Department of Labor reports.

Yet, Growth with a capital G is the inflationist battle cry. Without continuous inflation of the money volume and of prices, growth is supposed to stop, stagnation to set in. However, growthmanship promotes not progress, but just the opposite. Again, Dr. Mills' figures speak for themselves: Periods of "growth" were characterized by "retardation" in the rate of productivity's increase. The records of the nineteenth century support the same thesis. "During that remarkable period of economic growth from 1873 to 1893, when material wealth increased by about 140%, prices *decreased* more than 40%."[3] In fact, an artificially stimulated, rapid "growth" may be accompanied by a high level of unemployment. In 1937, under inflationary stimuli, the industrial production index hit the 1929 record—with eight million unemployed roaming the streets.

It is futile to ignore the sufferings and waste caused by the depression (as is done by a school of self-styled libertarians of the laissez faire variety). Equally futile is it to ignore the fact that every depression is the outgrowth of the preceding boom. Had the "recovery" maintained its natural path of *balanced growth*, it could have lasted indefinitely. *Monetary stability*, combined with sound fiscal and banking practices, *is the prime condition of economic progress*. It is the exaggeration and unbalancing of the process—overexpansions, physical and financial, leading to overemployment and other bottlenecks—that carry the penalty of a crash.[4] Exactly this state is what inflation brings about by obstructing

THE "PHILOSOPHY" OF INFLATION

sound entrepreneurial and investment judgments and whetting the political appetites.

The incessant clamor of the inflationist is that the gross national product (estimated total spending) must GROW every year at a fixed rate, be it 3 per cent, 4 per cent, or 5 per cent, the number varying according to his whim. There must be no letdown in the number game, no interruption, and it makes no difference on what we spend. The GNP never rises as it did in World Wars I and II; in the single year 1943 it jumped as much as 15 per cent, "thanks" to all the spending on military hardware. (Actually, in 1939 Keynes offered the British the flippant consolation that the destruction caused by the war would be to their benefit, creating employment and income thereafter.) But no cars and no homes were produced and shortages were the order of the day. There was *ample statistical growth,* but *very little economic progress.* The former is a matter of more money outpour; the latter, of real wealth creation.

Could it be that the ghost of the oldest of economic fallacies haunts the ivory towers of the academy, confusing money and real wealth, the lubricant and the source of energy? Or is it merely a case of economic myopia, the inability to see the consequences of monetary tympany beyond the immediate ebullience it evokes? In any event, the gross falsehood of the growth-at-any-price philosophy makes one suspect there must be ulterior motives behind it. There are, indeed, as we shall see.

1. In the past, periods of rising and falling prices alternated. The British retail price index of basic consumer goods fell by 51 per cent between 1813 and 1893; by 59 per cent between 1920 and 1932. E. H. Phelps Brown and Sheila V. Hopkins, "Seven Centuries of the Prices of Consumables, Compared with Builders' Wage-rates," *Economica*, Vol. XXIII, No. 92.

2. F. C. Mills, "The Role of Productivity in Economic Growth," *American Economic Review*, May, 1952.

3. R. T. Patterson, in *Commercial and Financial Chronicle*, August 20, 1959.

4. About overindebtedness, typical of every rash of speculative mania, see subsequent chapters.

VIII
CREEPING INFLATION AND INTELLECTUAL HONESTY

HOW MUCH IS A LITTLE?

Just how much inflation is a little inflation? This is the first question to which the proponents of creeping inflation must give an unequivocal answer as a matter of intellectual honesty. Their answers vary within a wide range.

Professor Jacob Viner of Princeton University, and one of Roosevelt's brain trust, pontificated:

> I shall begin to get scared, myself, if the rate at which prices rise on the average exceeds 10 per cent per annum. A one per cent increase per month, continuing over a period of months, in the wholesale price index, if not justification for hysteria is perhaps justification for alarm; if not for alarm, then certainly for grave concern.—*Commerce*, April, 1941.

One may wonder about the present state of mind of the eminent economist: scared, hysterical, alarmed, gravely concerned, or not concerned at all? But his wartime ruminations should not be taken too seriously. At that time, the upside-down economics of J. M. Keynes reigned supreme, in particular the theory that the saver is the destructive villain in the drama of the business cycle, the spender the constructive benefactor.

AN INFLATION PRIMER

Since rising prices penalize the wicked saver and stimulate the brave spender, it was rather conservative to be "concerned" about such a trifle as a monthly rate of price inflation exceeding one per cent.

Professor Paul A. Samuelson[1] of Massachusetts Institute of Technology, author of a widely used college textbook, in an early edition announced ex cathedra that *5 per cent* is the desirable rate of annual depreciation of the dollar's purchasing power. He was down to *2 per cent* per year in the 1958 edition, with no explanation for the change of heart. At this rate of progress of his own theory's depreciation, he may land—on the gold standard.

So far as the public is concerned, the late Harvard Professor Sumner H. Slichter was the prophet of creeping inflation. He seemed to mean a 3–5 per cent annual rise of prices. The *New York Times* of April 27, 1959, took him to task for "strange discrepancies between the Professor's statistics and the conclusions that their author draws from them," intimating that, having built up a clientele by forecasting perpetual inflation, he had acquired a vested interest in his own forecasts. (He propagandized spending and debt-monetizing policies that would have helped his forecasts to come true.) Slichter, in the *Commercial & Financial Chronicle* of July 23, 1959, reacted with intellectual somersaults. Instead of

CREEPING INFLATION

blaming the Federal Reserve for "creating unemployment," as he did only a few months earlier, he became its defender, putting the blame on the pressure groups, meaning the farmers and veterans. He still glorified the inflation that did marvels at the modest rate of 8 per cent in nine years. In other words, *less than 1 per cent* inflation per annum is sufficient to maintain prosperity, according to Slichter's last turn. We would not venture to divine the next turn of his famulus at Harvard, Professor J. Kenneth Galbraith.

CUTTING THE DOG'S TAIL PIECEMEAL

The answer to the first question, "How much is a little?" is anyone's guess, and the propagators of creeping inflation are not even bound by their own estimates, which have no scientific rationale whatsoever.

The second question should be equally embarrassing to the creeping inflationist. He posits some *annual percentage rate* of the money's future depreciation. Does he mean the same rate each year? That, of course, would be contrary to all experience. But a long-term *average* may be arrived at by a practically infinite number of combinations of annual rates. The sameness of the arithmetical result is no proof of identical economic meaning. Annual averages over a decade may take us back to the ups and downs of the old-fashioned boom-and-bust cycle.

Slichter admitted the obvious, namely that periods of boom alternate with years or months of recession. But then his creeping inflation boils down to short cycles of over- and underemployment, with a long-term bias in favor of higher prices.

Our third question also implies a test of the inflationist's intellectual honesty. How long is the "perpetual" creeping supposed to go on? For a limited period? Indefinitely? Forever? The answer, if any, is vague, evasive, noncommittal. Yet, this *is* crucial. If there is a reasonable time limit, the "fun" is spoiled. If there is none, people will notice sooner or later what they have to expect and will hedge against it by rushing to buy things before the money loses much of its purchasing power. Would that not turn the creeping inflation into the runaway or self-inflaming kind, a contingency to which our inflationists are opposed tooth and nail? According to Dr. Slichter, there is no such danger. Experience shows (to his satisfaction) that people take a cleverly planned or dosed inflation in stride and scarcely notice it, like the proverbial dog that would not suffer if its tail were cut by small pieces only.

On what assumptions is this diagnosis of human behavior based? On the ability of economists and politicians to bamboozle an ignorant public? But the propagandists themselves, of all people, are

CREEPING INFLATION

guilty of making people aware of the inflation. This is an extraordinary case of a forecaster whose forecast is doomed by his own efforts. If he convinced many of us that perpetual inflation is in the cards, we would be anxious to act on that knowledge—to buy, borrow, and speculate on further rising markets, spelling finis to the slow inflation. Slichter might have had a better chance of being proved right if he had stopped tooting his prognostications from the literary housetops.

The unions understood that the dilution of the currency creates a redundancy of demand. Supply cannot catch up at once. A prime limiting factor is the relative shortage of qualified labor; on that, labor "bargaining" thrives. But rising wages unleash vicious spirals, which in turn upset the neat calculations of the planners. Small wonder that Slichter was growing increasingly critical about the unions. They were ruining *his* balderdash—by acting on *his* theory of slow inflation. Instead of recognizing the effect of his own mischievious and inconsistent propaganda, he cried out that the community should not "tolerate this topsy-turvy system of distribution" by which "labor exploits capital, science, and engineering."[2]

The trouble with planned inflation, slow or otherwise, is that inflation cannot be planned. Planners (technocrats) think of running a social organism as a mechanical contraption. This is a naive concept of the body economic—of human nature. By controlling the flow of fuel, one controls the speed of the motor. By regulating the flow of spendable funds, the planners propose to control the flow of demand for consumer and capital goods, and this without serious interruptions. However, the motor does not discount the *future* intake of fuel; men do anticipate the forthcoming action of the monetary authorities if they know or think they know it in advance with reasonable certainty. This is exactly what slow inflation brings about, *once the pattern is definitely established* in people's minds.

POWER VERSUS FREEDOM

In a free or relatively free economy inflation cannot be planned, but a planned economy cannot operate without inflation. Even the almighty Soviets live under its constant pressure (interrupted periodically by brutal deflationary measures). The same is true for the patronage state—misnamed welfare state—in which maintaining the national budget and the credit system in a sound operating condition and conserving the internal as well as the external stability of the currency are secondary considerations, at best. Under the rule of the gold standard, the money supply is "disciplined." So is the budget, because the Treasury's recourse to the printing press is restrained. Then, too, the politicians' *power* to plan or to manage the economy and to pour out patronage is restrained. (The law of corruption: corruption grows in geometric proportion to the volume of public expenditures.) Herein lies the crux of the whole monetary debate. In ultimate analysis, it boils down to the *choice between a free, competitive-market economy and a statist or collectivist system run by political fiat.*

Currency manipulation is not only a characteristic of every collectivist society; it is the safest and surest way to collectivize every society. "The issue between individualism and collectivism, between internationalism and economic nationalism, is settled when a country has decided what kind of monetary system it is going to have. If the government is free to manufacture and manipulate money at will and arbitrarily, then we cease to have a free society."[3]

Openly or in disguise, the proponent of collectivist policies starts from the assumption that the price mechanism fails to perform its essential functions. (See Chapter VII.) If he does not negate the free-enterprise system altogether, he is at any rate highly skeptical about its efficiency or desirability. That system deprives him of chances to exercise *real power,* power over production and distribution. Hence, the claim that the government has to take over where business allegedly leaves off. Full employment (no-more-depression) was one patent pretext written into the statutes, if only in vague wording, as the Employment Act of 1946. But contracyclical meddling turns out to be inflationary, so the next step is to add insult to injury by requesting that price stability should also be guaranteed—by the government. Lately, the public is deluged with the official and unofficial promotion of growth as the overriding value to justify more public spending, taxing, inflating, and meddling.

The theories and techniques change, but the object is constant: to win many friends and influence many voters. Short of military victory, nothing serves the ambitious politician better than the appeal (in humanitarian lingo, of course) to the greed of groups with substantial weight at the polls. Crawling inflation is a very convenient avenue for the *redistribution* of incomes and wealth, a most effective subsidiary to discriminatory taxation, political patronage, governmental meddling, and outright corruption. Even the tightrope act of "balancing" the economy between booms and recessions necessitates a host of incisive fiscal and monetary maneuvers. And should the inflation get out of hand, the collectivist stands ready with price, profit, and wage controls, allocations, rationing, credit controls, foreign-exchange barbed wires, and nationalizations. The greater the calamity brought about by the inflation, the broader the power he is likely to acquire to combat the inflation by "physical" (bureaucratic) methods of repression.

MUST WE FOLLOW THE KREMLIN?

A word about the collectivist is appropriate. He is no Communist, oh no! Frequently, he claims to be a believer in economic freedom, with a bit of money management superimposed. But on some basic points his thinking happens to coincide with the Kremlin line. Growth at any price, his ultimate ideal, is straight out of the bolshevist horse's mouth. And (changing the metaphor) he rides that horse for all it is worth.

Russia's propaganda about her progress—measured in imaginative price data—is being held up for boundless admiration. Never mind that the data are notoriously faked, or that the Soviets know little and care less about their own costs;[4] they can always reduce living standards, in addition to wasting their own and their satellites' resources. The sophomoric notion of a Russia that lacks the incentives and a rational price system, the touchstones of efficiency, overtaking us is being dangled as a Damocles sword. (If she did, everyone, including ourselves, would be better off.) For years, she is supposed to be on the verge of flooding the world's export markets, although the dollar volume of her exports to non-Soviet countries never reaches that of Switzerland or

Sweden. Such irrational propaganda serves also to justify our foreign-aid outpour.

The Western ("democratic") collectivist and the Eastern (totalitarian) communist have more in common than either would care to admit. The common concept of monetary and credit manipulation is but one expression of an ideology that is the very opposite of economic freedom—which means free choice by the consumer. On the free market, the consumer's vote reigns sovereign in determining what should be produced. His satisfaction, the rise of his living standard, is the acid test of progress. To that, collectivists and communists pay lip service; but their fetish, growth, is something else. Their emphasis is not on individual *consumer wants*, but on collective *"public" needs*. As is well known, the Soviets give primacy to armaments and capital goods; the average consumer gets a minimum of benefits, with very limited choice. A superbureaucracy does the choosing. That is very nearly the idea our statists are pursuing, with a difference in degree due to the difference in political climate.

As the powers that be enlarge their grip over the nation's income and resources, they substitute progressively their own judgments for consumer choices. Inescapably, "welfare" turns into patronage. The volume of investment, instead of accommodating itself to available savings, is subject to inflationary expansion.[5] All this vastly

CREEPING INFLATION

enlarges the radius of governmental and pressure-group action, arbitrarily confounding, or revolutionizing, the distribution of incomes and the pattern of industrial development. Whether the rationalization is to overcome the alleged inequities of capitalism and its inherent "stagnation," to create more employment, or to promote growth, the result is to shift the management from the hands of entrepreneurs, who are responsible to the verdict of the market, into the arms of technocrats responsible to politicians, if at all. Even under the unrealistic assumption that the planners are incorruptible, mismanagement is the outcome, unless they are superhuman and know better what is good for the consumer than he does himself and make no major errors in guessing the future of the markets.

Where the logic of collectivist yearning drifts is perfectly illustrated by its recent turn against the "affluent society," meaning the free choice by the consumer. Leaders of the "liberal" intelligentsia have lately been producing best sellers purporting to show that we (and the British cousins) are living too high on the hog, badly neglecting the poor fellow, the government—who happens to absorb directly up to 30 per cent of the national income and who manages or distorts a great deal more by remote controls, especially by inflation.

In the forefront of this neocollectivist move-

81

ment will be found outstanding "liberals" of the Keynes-Slichter school of inflationism: Harvard Professor J. Kenneth Galbraith, economist of the Democrats for Political Action (the brain trust of the Democratic Party's union-supported left wing), and his British counterpart, Richard Crossman, a spokesman of the Labor Party, or of its Left. This is not accidental. The inflationist intent is, fundamentally, to stultify the autonomy of the market and to foster the growth of the government's power. Sooner or later, the power motive in the back of the inflationist mind breaks into the open. It may be through the curtain of tears shed for the hungry millions in the underdeveloped countries (and their socialist planners), for whose benefit we are to be forced into involuntary AUSTERITY, a new catchword for the old idea of equalizing incomes (downward).

Creeping inflation and galloping socialism are ideologic brothers under the skin. They complement each other in the pursuit of unhappiness—of more regulating and spending authority for the government. "Eggheads" may be inflationists, but collectivists are no dreamers. They know what they want. Inflation, to them, is not self-purpose; it is one instrument among others to gain and hold power. When inflation ceases to make friends, nay, threatens with popular reaction against the collectivist trend, yesterday's easy-going inflationist turns into tomorrow's stern moralist.

1. During the 1960 presidential campaign, he was a top economic advisor to the Democratic candidate.

2. Virtually in the same breath, Slichter paid tribute to the unions' excessive wage demands as an "independent cause of the [1959] recovery."

3. Philip Cortney, in *The New York Times,* December 10, 1949.

4. Even by their own inflated figures (their dairy output includes the milk consumed by the calves), the Soviets' rate of growth is declining: from an average annual 14.1 per cent in 1949-53 to 7.7 per cent in 1957-1959. By 1960 it was trailing far behind that year's 12 per cent industrial output growth in the European Common Market. Soviet statistics have been deflated lately by one of Russia's own top-level economists (*New York Times,* September 11, 1960).

5. "A myth of expansion [is] a way of attenuating, by public intervention, the sterilizing effect of inflation, of excessive taxation, and of the erosion of savings."—Jacques Rueff, outstanding French economist.

IX

INFLATION'S BALANCE SHEET: THE LIABILITIES

PROGRESS BY INFLATION

Statisticians compile data which add up to the much-revered figure called the national income. Planners plan by that figure, supposedly, setting targets for its growth. Many economists and many more politicians use it as the infallible yardstick of the nation's progress, wealth, and welfare. To the inflationists, the growth of the magic figure is the supreme objective of policy. It has been rising, indeed, an accomplishment they claim is made possible, if not actually created, by the brimful money supply. Without that, there would be Stagnation, with a capital S.

Now, the national income is a somewhat less than reliable "aggregate." The data

> ... about the components entering into such aggregates as national income, volume of production, savings and investment, etc., are pure "guesstimates," subject to arbitrary manipulation. The methods to substitute what amounts to "very wild guesses" in the place of factual knowledge are known to the statisticians as "interpolating between benchmarks, extrapolating from benchmarks, blowing up sample data, using imputed weights, inserting trends, applying booster factors. . . ." According to out-

INFLATION'S BALANCE SHEET: THE LIABILITIES

standing British statisticians, "The result (of forecasts based on national income statistics) looks about as scientific as Alice's celebrated attempt to play croquet by hitting a live hedgehog with a flamingo."[1]

For the sake of argument, let us accept the concept, vague and hazy as it is, at face value. The gross national income's rate of progress since 1950 has been unusual, averaging some 5 per cent a year in dollars of depreciating purchasing power. Translated into "real" income by eliminating the price-inflation factor, this means a rise of about 3.2 per cent annually, which is roughly the same average that obtained in the thirty-four-year period 1880–1914, under stable money, through several booms, crises, and depressions. Did we need the stimuli of managed money, unbalanced budgets, creeping price inflation, huge armaments, fantastic price props, a cornucopia of domestic and foreign subsidies, and a multitude of bureaucratic interventions—all of which involves a great deal of waste and corruption—to accomplish what we have done before without such shots-in-the-arm?

That is not all. What matters is the per capita growth rather than the total growth. Per capita, given the rapid rise of population, the *real* national income rises by little more than 1 per cent a year. Even of this modest increase, a large portion produces no economic values. About one-fourth of the increase originates in military expenditures, governmental stockpiles of unsalable commodities, "unproductive" services of bureaucrats, and the like. The *true* (per capita) growth of goods and services available for the satisfaction of the consumer or for additions to the nation's productive capacity may be three-fourths of 1 per cent per annum, or less, far below the comparable late nineteenth-century record. In fact, it is well below the record of the period 1920–28, a period of stable prices and of a comparatively slow rate of population growth.

For illustration: in 1958, the average American family's income is supposed to have "risen" by—$20, or one-third of 1 per cent, this before taxes.

Such is the much-advertised growth of our national income, the asset side of creeping inflation's balance sheet. The liability side is being ignored, deliberately.

THE LIABILITY SIDE

There is a price to be paid for an artificially engineered growth. For one thing, with every 1 per cent increase of the national income, our debts, net after elimination of duplications, grow by 1.7 per cent. This they did in the 1920's, too. This "growth" is spectacular, indeed, as shown in the table on the facing page.

Between 1950 and 1958, the *net nonfederal debt* of the American people has risen *five times*

INFLATION'S BALANCE SHEET: THE LIABILITIES

faster than during the corresponding eight years of the lusty 1920's. True, in the current period the dollar's purchasing power has been cut severely, while it was stable in the previous one. Even if the figures are corrected accordingly, the rise in the current boom has been proceeding at a rate almost treble that in the previous great prosperity.

Note that in the 1920's the net governmental debt remained stable; the federal government liquidated (repaid!) as much as the state and local authorities borrowed. In the 1950's, both went into the red. *For every one-dollar increase of the total net debt in the twenties, we added seven dollars in the fifties.*

"NET" DEBT OUTSTANDING
(in Billions of Dollars)

End of Year	Governmental Federal*	Governmental State and local	Private Corporate	Private Individual†	Total
1921......	$ 23.1	$ 6.5	$ 57.0	$ 49.2	$135.8
1925......	20.3	10.0	72.7	59.6	162.6
1929......	16.5	13.2	88.9	72.3	190.9
1940......	44.8	16.5	75.6	53.0	189.9
1946......	229.7	13.6	93.5	60.6	397.4
1950......	218.7	20.7	142.1	109.2	490.7
1954......	230.2	33.4	177.5	165.4	606.5
1958......	232.7	50.9	255.7	240.4	779.7
1959......	243.2	55.6	281.7	265.8	846.4
Change:					
1921–29...	− 6.6	+ 6.4	+ 31.9	+ 23.1	+ 55.1
1929–40...	+ 28.3	+ 3.3	− 13.3	− 19.3	− 1.0
1940–59...	+198.4	+39.1	+206.1	+212.8	+656.5

*The *true* federal debt is about $40 billion larger than the "net" figure. See Chapter X.
†Includes noncorporate enterprises.

AN INFLATION PRIMER

The major portion of the funds to finance the inflation of the personal debt—a credit expansion that fans the fire under the price level—stems from the banks and the savings associations. By the end of 1958 they carried, between them, over 60 per cent of the outstanding mortgage loans on one- to four-family homes. Directly and by indirection, the *commercial banks* also provide the bulk of installment credit (up to three years), this on top of a growing volume of business term loans (up to ten years!) and "slow" loans to business, plus substantial holdings of medium- and long-term corporate and municipal bonds. The obvious hazards involved in overloaning themselves and in impairing the liquidity of the earning assets seem to be ignored by a new generation of bankers. This new generation does not remember the depression and is being sold, just like the fathers were thirty-odd years ago, on the idea that there never will be another.

BORROWING A LIVING STANDARD

Presently, the most rapidly rising component of the credit structure is the "individual" debt of nonfarm households and unincorporated businesses. This debt grows a great deal faster than the personal disposable income after deduction of direct taxes, as shown in the next table.

In 1959, the net addition to the outstanding personal debt alone (mortgages on one- to four-

INFLATION'S BALANCE SHEET: THE LIABILITIES

family nonfarm residential buildings plus consumer loans) was $19.4 billion, a record. Installment credit is currently expanding at the annual rate of $5.5 billion, or 9 per cent, also a record. As consumers, we are pre-empting expected future income. Evidently, our per-capita consumption could not improve even at the modest annual rate the statistics show if it were not bolstered by purchases on credit that will limit our future consumption. But for the time being, such purchases permit a standard of living above the level of earnings.

How long this process of piling up debts in excess of incomes—and ahead of the rate at which liquid savings are built up—can continue, no one knows. But no one in his right senses would dare to assert that it can go on indefinitely, or without serious interruption. Every minor interruption means a recession; a major one spells depression. Thus, *instability is being built into a supposedly depression-proof economy.*

End of Year	Disposable Personal Income (billions)	Gain, %	Net Individual and Noncorporate Debt (billions)	Gain, %
1950	$207.7	..	$108.9	..
1951	227.5	10	119.8	9
1952	238.7	5	135.6	12
1953	252.5	7	150.4	10
1954	256.9	2	165.4	9
1955	274.4	7	190.2	13
1956	292.9	6	207.5	8
1957	307.9	5	221.9	6
1958	316.5	3	239.7	7
1959	334.6	5	265.1	10

At that, the comparison of total disposable income with the total of personal debt does not give the right picture. The one is accruing to the population as a whole; the other is owed by a section of the population only—surely not by millionaires. According to a recent Federal Reserve Board survey, 32 per cent of all "spending units" (families) had no debt at all; of the indebted 68 per cent, two-fifths were obligated both ways, by consumer loans as well as by mortgages. The economic visionaries who dream of eternal prosperity, or of perpetual creeping inflation which is the same mirage, derive satisfaction from the fact that not all families are burdened with personal debts. In reality, this is very ominous. It means that, for a majority, the annual increase of the debt is outpacing the annual growth of disposable income. What will be the proportion, say, *five or ten years hence*, if the inflation "creeps" that long?

The debt obsession, induced by the excessive money supply and nurtured by an inflationary psychology, produces paradoxical phenomena. In 1959, personal debt creation proceeded apace despite the steel strike. After three months without visible income, the credit of the striking steelworkers seemed better than ever. In Gary, the local businesses offered the steelworkers almost everything, from socks and pants to furniture and videos—at no down payment. Just take the goods

INFLATION'S BALANCE SHEET: THE LIABILITIES

and sign a piece of paper; the paper was eligible as collateral for a bank loan. The disproportion between current production and current consumption is highlighted by this example of unemployed labor maintaining its spending habits in anticipation of a wage increase. But it would take decades for any increase to make up for the wages lost during the strike, let alone the installments on the new debts, with 10 per cent annual interest charge in the "bargain."

Nothing wrong with buying homes on credit, with ever less down payments needed and ever more interest charged for stretched-out periods, the dreamers argue (in waking hours). The families merely pay for mortgages, plus upkeep and tax, what they would otherwise have paid for rent. Maybe so, in some cases, but for a majority, it takes an irresponsible optimism to ignore the pitfalls. Construction cost per dwelling unit tends to decrease with the number of dwellings under one roof, and so does the rent. Home ownership may be desirable for many reasons, but it can be a serious obstacle to the worker-owner's mobility and earning power or to his ability to adapt himself to changing conditions.

Again, the problem is not so much the present size of the home-mortgage debt; the problem is—where do we go from here? Can people afford, and *how much longer* can they afford, to mortgage themselves at the annual rate of $10 billion to $15 billion far in advance of the growth of their incomes? What of the creditors, if anything should go wrong? Nothing to worry about, take the word of N. H. Jacoby, a former member of the President's Council of Economic Advisors:

> While home mortgage and consumer debt has quintupled since 1946, we must recall that family incomes, assets, and equities in homes have grown proportionately. Sixty per cent of American families live in homes they own, and half of these homes are free of mortgage debt. Moreover, nearly 40 per cent of all home mortgage loans are VA-*guaranteed* or FHA-*insured*—55 billion of the 114 billion outstanding. With currently low default and delinquency ratios on mortgage debt, there appears to be *no danger* in this quarter. [Italics ours.]—*Commercial and Financial Chronicle,* October 8, 1959.

There is "no danger" of future defaults *because* there are no defaults now, while the money is pouring out of the banking system and confidence (in coming inflation) is unshaken. Such irresistible logic is typical of the economic tranquilizers produced by thinking in "aggregates." Of course, the "aggregate" volume of mortgages may never go in default, but the story may be different for those mortgages incurred at high cost in purchasing speculatively overvalued properties.[2] As it is, banks and savings institutions rarely find the names of their home-mortgage debtors on the ledgers of their savings accounts.

The ultimate tranquilizer is: falling back on Uncle Sam. He insures or guarantees, as just

INFLATION'S BALANCE SHEET: THE LIABILITIES

quoted, $55 billion of $144 billion outstanding home-mortgage loans. That still leaves $90 billion unprotected, even if the U.S. Treasury, hopelessly entangled in its debt problems, should be able to take care of additional billions worth of bonds with which to satisfy the mortgage creditors. These additional bonds would be either thrown on an overloaded capital market or monetized by the banks. By that time, a "new" kind of creeping inflation may be under way, one accompanied by stagnation.

Of course, the American economy has grown "larger" and richer in a generation's lifetime; it can take (swallow?) more debts. But it has not grown three times larger; it did not even double in productive capacity. Still less can its further growth keep up with the accelerating growth of the debt.

Needless to say, crises and panics do not require that all debtors go bankrupt. The bankruptcy of a modest fraction does it. At present, far more than a modest fraction of consumers is better than knee-deep in debts,[3] and going ever deeper. "Growth" of this kind surely may raise living standards now; just as surely, someone's living standards may have to suffer later. Indeed, *austerity*—restraint in consumption—is what some inflationists advocate already.

Fortunately, the market forces, if permitted to operate, tend to bring about an automatic correc-

AN INFLATION PRIMER

tion of the borrowing and spending excesses. The expansion of personal loans is a significant factor in tightening the banks' lending capacity and raising the interest rates. This puts a damper on the supply of credit, provided the Federal Reserve goes slowly with its anticyclical medicaments to rehabilitate the organized recklessness.

Business corporations and local authorities contribute their share to the debt inflation. Between 1930 and 1959, the short-term debt of nonfinancial corporations other than railroads has quadrupled, and their long-term debt has more than trebled. Probably some 15 per cent of the latter is due annually. Interest charges did not rise proportionately, thanks to lower rates and to the tax-deductibility feature; but the profit margin per sales dollar declined, too, in the 1950's, and the tax collector takes 52 per cent of the net. So, the *debt burden of corporations,* relative to their net (after taxes), has *greatly increased* and their expansion potential has been curtailed, to say nothing of the impending threat of illiquidity.

That this process is not fraught with very serious hazards can be believed only by those who have taken out a patent on eternal prosperity, a world in which debts are owed to one's own "pocket."

"PEOPLE'S CAPITALISM"

Specious fruits grow on the tree of creeping

INFLATION'S BALANCE SHEET: THE LIABILITIES

inflation. One of them is being hailed as "people's capitalism," meaning the fantastic proliferation of stockholders in and out of investment trusts. Investment trusts play the market with billions of dollars, most of it put up by people who have no business risking their modest savings in ventures of which they know nothing. It is the lusty 1920's all over again, with the same ruthless techniques in exploiting ignorance and greed and the same breed of "financiers" pocketing untold fortunes. The latter plead perfect innocence, of course. What's wrong with getting rich? Nothing, provided the deal is not unfairly "loaded" and the customer does not get hurt when the day of "reckoning" (in sensible price-earning ratios) arises. A chief source of the anticapitalistic sentiment of the 1930's, to which we owe the New Deal and the welfare state, was exactly the same "innocent" practice. When millions of people lose their money on gambling, on which they were sold as if it were legitimate business, they turn against the whole system that supplied the gambling chances, and the money cranks have a heyday.

This is different from the 1920's, the salesmen of sloth assure us. Then, people gambled on borrowed money; when the market fell, they were wiped out. Nothing of the sort is threatening now when all they might lose in a crash (which never, never will happen again) is their own savings (as if that would make them feel much better).

Margin requirements, reduced from 90 to 70 per cent, virtually prohibit speculative excesses. Look at the figures of brokers' loans: they are a mere fraction of what they were in 1929, compared with the dollar volume of stock-exchange transactions then and now. Moreover, the public cannot be deceived any more, thanks to strict controls by the Securities and Exchange Commission, several national and fifty state agencies, and the stock exchanges themselves.

Most of this belongs in the category of "eye wash." The authorities may check palpable fraud but have no power over intangible, possibly bona fide, mal-persuasion. A vast volume of shares, quoted on the over-the-counter market, are not even subject to margin requirements. As for the margin borrower, he gives written assurance to the banker that he is not using the credit for purchasing or holding securities, but there is no control, no effective penalty on circumventing the law.

And debt subterfuges are being concocted. The worker at the bench and the farmer in the barn are being parleyed into signing up for ten years or longer on fixed-sum annual plans to purchase investment-trust certificates. They can cancel the plan, but the cost of doing so is prohibitive. In all but name, the buyer incurs a debt that is not registered in the statistics of debts.

Easy money "eases" the moral fiber of society.

INFLATION'S BALANCE SHEET: THE LIABILITIES

When government housekeeping is oblivious of the rules of economy, private households are strongly tempted to follow the same pattern. When acquiring wealth becomes a matter of gambling and politicking, as it does in the inflation morass, real values are likely to suffer. Witness the proliferation of criminality, embezzlement, and tax evasion, symptoms of the disease that has its prime roots in monetary and fiscal policies. The drawn-out depreciation of the currency's purchasing power cannot fail to affect standards other than the monetary alone.

Inflation, and the spirit which nourishes it and accepts it, is merely the monetary aspect of the general decay of law and of respect for law. It requires no special astuteness to realize that the vanishing respect for property is very intimately related to the numbing of respect for the integrity of money and its value. In fact, laxity about property and laxity about money are very closely bound up together; in both cases what is firm, durable, earned, secured, and designed for continuity gives place to what is fragile, fugitive, fleeting, unsure, and ephemeral. And that is not the kind of foundation on which the free society can long remain standing.—Professor Wilhelm Roepke, Geneva, Switzerland.

1. From this writer's book, *Managed Money at the Crossroads* (Notre Dame, Ind.: University of Notre Dame Press, 1958), pp. 136-7.

2. Too often, twenty- and thirty-year mortgages finance homes that may have to be rebuilt in fifteen years.

3. According to a 1960 Federal Reserve survey, "Close to 20% of all spending units were devoting 20% or more of their disposable income to installment payments." But a good deal of the "disposable" income is not disposable at all.

X

THE BURDEN OF THE NATIONAL DEBT

IS IT A BURDEN ON THE NATION?

It is not, provided it is being held domestically, proclaimed President Franklin D. Roosevelt. "One pocket owes it to the other." (Debt owed to foreigners is considered as belonging in another chapter.) Since the public debt is no debt in the common meaning of the term, it need not be and virtually never has been repaid, according to the managed-money and creeping-inflation advocates. We should learn to live with the mammoth debt and accept the alleged necessity of its further growth. Let us go on accumulating budget deficits whenever "needed." Consider the size of the pile as irrelevant. As a Harvard professor announced it not long ago: it makes no difference whether the federal debt is $300 billion [nine zeros] or $300 trillion [twelve zeros]. Why, far from being a national liability in a meaningful sense, it might be considered as a wealth-creating asset. How could one enjoy all the "blessings" of currency-diluting if it were not for the debt and its recurrent monetization? How would we overcome depressions (in the midst of booms), maintain full employment, and spend ourselves into ever greater richness? He who believes in inflation as a panacea for curing social ills, or even as a necessary evil, must justify the existence and growth of the overextended national debt.

But the principle of "one pocket owes it to the other" applies to a communistic society only. When everything belongs to the state, all liabilities are a matter of mere bookkeeping. Conversely, he who denies that the debt is more than a bookkeeping item, wittingly or unwittingly, negates the system of private property. Under that system, the "pockets" of creditors are distinctly separate from those of debtors. A gain of the one is no compensation for a loss to the other.

Yet, the "two-pockets" principle asserts that, in contrast to private debts, servicing the public debt merely means a transfer of income from one group to the other. Real resources are not affected. "The fact that the government owes its citizens certain sums is not really a burden on the nation as a whole," asserted *The Economist* (London) of November 21, 1959. That would be true if a 100 per cent tax were levied on income derived from federal securities. Of course, no one would buy the bonds, except the Federal Reserve that delivers to the Treasury practically all earnings on its huge portfolio.

Presently, the American taxpayer is burdened with $9 billion a year for interest on the $290 billion debt, nearly twelve cents of every dollar of federal revenue. Are we to believe that we would be no better off if federal taxes were 12 per cent lower, even though the bondholders would receive that much less? (Could they not have invested in other securities?) By the same token, no tax ever is a burden, provided the money taken from a domestic Peter is "transferred" to a domestic Paul, which is what usually happens.

Note how neatly the argument for the public debt's alleged economic innocence fits into the not-so-innocent frame of mind of the demagogues who plead for wealth redistribution. Why not indulge in such "transfers" by which the loss of one side is compensated, supposedly, by profits of the other? By promoting the something-for-nothing illusion, debt-making serves not only as the motor of inflation, but also as an intellectual vehicle of collectivism.

THE ECONOMICS OF THE DEBT

The interest charge on the national debt is a strategic element in the federal budget. Without the $9 billion—minus $3 billion, maybe, allowing for the bondholder's income tax, etc.—among the "overhead" costs of government, the budget could be held in balance and the debt reduced by a notch, still leaving some funds available for tax cuts.

The national debt burdens the economy in

THE BURDEN OF THE NATIONAL DEBT

more than one way. New money the government borrows is taken out of the nation's "pool" of savings: $7 billion in 1958, $5 billion in 1959. That much less is left to other borrowers—business, consumers, local authorities, home builders. A shortage of capital is engendered and interest rates mount, raising production costs and living costs in addition to the government's own costs of operation.

For another thing, what did the government do with the money? Little, if any, has been invested in a productive fashion. Wherever it went, almost none flows back. Its interest charges are not covered by forthcoming earnings, as in the case of reproductive (self-liquidating) investment. Instead, the charges have to be paid out of taxes, which are paid largely by lower-middle-class people engaged in production, and a disincentive is fostered.

Some of the borrowing was necessary, to be sure. It is scarcely possible for current revenues to cover all war expenditures. But even during wars, the abandon with which the responsible politicians plunge into irresponsible borrowing—of the most dangerous short-term variety, preferably—is something to behold. What justification is there in this prosperous postwar era for not reducing the debt, nay, for raising it further?

Of course, it is much easier to win support for public spending out of future generations' income than at the living, and voting, taxpayers' expense. The latter resent higher taxation, especially when the burden is very heavy already, while the former cannot talk back. By recourse to borrowing, a singular hurdle to foolhardy projects (with popular appeal) is eliminated. And something else is eliminated: the rational control over the use of the borrowed funds. As Adam Smith wrote nearly 200 years ago, speaking of the difference between private and public debt:

> A creditor of the public, considered merely as such, has no interest in the good condition of any particular portion of land, or in the good management of any particular portion of capital stock. As a creditor of the public he has no knowledge of any such particular portion. He has no inspection of it. He can have no care about it. Its ruin may in some cases be unknown to him, and cannot directly affect him.

Budgetary controls are a highly unsatisfactory substitute for the lender's "inspection" of individual credit risks, least satisfactory on the postwar scene, when the Congress cannot even figure out the exact state of fiscal commitments, or the government its own operational condition. The federal budget is in a hopeless confusion, perpetuated by the demagogues' disposition to take credit for current welfare spending and leave the debit to their successors.

The sheer size of the American national debt should provide food for thought. Instead, it pro-

THE BURDEN OF THE NATIONAL DEBT

vides the inflationists with a hollow argument. Why, the "bankers" were hollering about national bankruptcy if the debt should pass $50 billion. Now, we are close to $300 billion, and the shouting has subsided. What matters is not the actual size of the debt but its proportion to the national income, ignoring the fact that the two rise together: more debt means more paper income. If the debt rises faster, that is no problem either. One simply declares that the new proportion *is* the right one. The richer the nation, the greater its ability to pay and the more it can borrow, a reasoning which at least recognizes that the debt is a burden. But it does not recognize the fact that in the process of accumulating the debt, prices had been inflated, the credit structure distorted, the savers shortchanged, the nation's financial standards corrupted, and the foundations of the free-enterprise system impaired. Misgivings of sane minds were due to the foresight that unsavory practices would have to be used in "selling" a blown-up volume of obligations, with a chain reaction of sickening repercussions to be expected.

FISCAL LEGERDEMAINS

Our national debt is equal to three-fifths of the annual gross national product, nearly double the public debts of all non-Soviet countries combined. How can the American capital market carry such a load of parasitical claims and still function? It

AN INFLATION PRIMER

does so by a number of financial tricks and deceptive devices, all contrary to the operational rules of the free market, some even to the criteria of the criminal code.

Let us consider the distribution of the debt by major categories of holders, starting with the some $50 billion in the Treasury's trust funds, largely the social security, the railroad pension, and the veterans' life insurance accounts. These funds represent the excess of special payroll taxes over and above the amounts disbursed. The managers of an insurance or of a trust company would soon be out of business if they invested in their own obligations the funds entrusted to them. But that is precisely what the government does. It diverts the earmarked revenues into general expenditures and puts its own IOU's in the respective accounts. It considers these well-"placed" obligations as owned by itself: the Treasury's one pocket owes it to the Treasury's other pocket. The sovereign cannot be put in his own penitentiary. In contrast, continental social-insurance systems, notably the German, are autonomous bodies that invest their reserves traditionally in bonds of private (regulated) mortgage-credit institutions—rather than in government obligations.

The interest on these well-placed bonds is "paid" in more IOU's. What if outgoing payments should exceed the contributions? Why, that is simple; the rate of the levy will be raised, or more people will be forced to take the "insurance." A more ingenious piece of financial legerdemain is hard to invent. Quite logically, the bureaucrats figure that, since agencies of Uncle Sam hold the obligations of Uncle Sam, the two sides of his ledger cancel out. Accordingly, $40-odd billion are deducted from the "gross" national debt. The "net" debt is reduced by that amount, thus adding a statistical legerdemain to the financial one. In any case, one-sixth of the debt is no headache to the Treasury (for the time being).

FALSIFYING THE BANK BALANCE SHEETS

There are several more dumping places for federal securities, namely, agencies that have no other choice in investing their funds, though they are not organs of the Treasury. Number one is the central bank. The Federal Reserve holds some $27 billion which, by and large, have to be "rolled over" from one maturity date to the next, depriving the Reserve System of its freedom of maneuvering. It buys bonds but scarcely ever sells a major amount.

Another revealing case in point is the Federal Deposit Insurance Corporation. This agency sinks the "insurance" premiums paid by the banks into long-term government bonds, accumulating so far about $2¼-billion worth, as a guaranty fund for some $140 billion of "insured" bank deposits. The FDIC itself brought out in its report for 1957 that, in effect, deposit insurance is relevant only in a bank crisis—in which case the FDIC would not be helpful at all. Its funds might be exhausted if a single one among the eight biggest banks would get into trouble, to say nothing of a widespread run. (The public's impression is that the deposits are guaranteed by the government, which is not the case.) On top of that, to cover even a small fraction of the "insured" deposits, the FDIC would have to liquidate its own holdings and break the bond market. Not only is this a phony arrangement which misleads the public, but it also misleads the banks to reckless credit policies and to negligence in building up proper capital accounts for the protection of the deposits. The banks rely on the "insurance"—and on their own holdings of government securities.

That brings us to the some $65 billion of federal securities held by the banking fraternity, equal at the end of 1959 (on the books) to about 25 per cent of total deposits. Insurance companies and savings and loan associations were holding another $20 billion. The institutions are under no compulsion to buy and are free to sell—legally. *De facto*, they have a limited choice only. They are cajoled (and bamboozled) into buying and retaining these securities, mostly of longer than one-year maturity, in violation of economic common sense, business ethics, and governmental responsibility.

A corporation publishing faked balance sheets

THE BURDEN OF THE NATIONAL DEBT

would be barred from every stock exchange. It may face criminal prosecution. The objective is to protect the investor against fraud. The same fraudulent practice, however, is legalized so far as commercial and savings banks are concerned. They can carry government bonds on their books at *par* value. A $1,000 bond may be quoted on the market at $800 or less; the balance sheet of your bank still may show it at $1,000. No need to write off such losses out of current profits. The banks may even pay dividends—out of losses.

The purpose of this perverted regulation, adopted by all federal and state supervisory agencies and by the SEC, is to give those bonds a sacrosanct status, guaranteed against book losses. Thereby, they are promoted to absolutely safe and "liquid" investments. The bank examiners count the federal bonds, whatever their maturity and actual price, as *prime liquid* assets, just like cash. The more bonds in the portfolio, the more liquid is the bank, by the examiners' standards, and never mind the losses. (The more loans, the less liquid is the bank, and never mind the quality or the maturity of the loans!)

Small wonder that the banks purchase risk-loaded long-term federal obligations, thereby creating a market for them. (They are easily "persuaded" to buy short-terms: the Treasury sweetens the deals by throwing deposits on tax-and-loan-accounts into the bargain.) With rising interest rates and declining values of medium- and long-term securities, as in 1958–59, the much too modest capital accounts, or reserves against losses, were impaired in most banks! In a number of banks, the entire capital and surplus had been lost. In some, even a part of the deposits was wiped out. The public knows nothing about this sad situation. No newspaper dares to discuss it, or the preposterous methods of the government at the root of it. The "silence of the sea" covers them up. Those persons on the inside (and with insight) hope and pray that a recession will reduce the pressure on the capital market, raise bond prices, and wipe out the losses. Very likely it will; but what about the next cycle? For how long, or how many times, will the depositors and savers permit themselves to be fooled? Sooner or later every legerdemain, subtle as it may be, is exposed and backfires.

As it is, the bond portfolios tend to "freeze in" time and again. By selling them, the banks disclose their losses, which would skyrocket if major amounts were liquidated. While the boom and high interest rates prevail, the "prime liquidity" turns into prime il-liquidity—unless the bonds are monetized by, and the losses shifted to, the Federal Reserve. The central bank may, perhaps, be relied on to resist the "temptation" to absorb either or both temptations, but it could be overruled by the Congress.

THE BURDEN OF THE NATIONAL DEBT

History may not teach anything (to those who do not wish to learn), but it certainly shows what happens to every public debt that has become burdensome. Sooner or later, it is liquidated. There are two kinds of illegitimate *liquidation*, in addition to the legitimate kind. State bankruptcy, the partial or total repudiation of capital or interest, or both, is one technique, a favorite pastime of totalitarian states. The other kind consists in a gradual depreciation of the currency, wiping out the real value (the burden!) of the obligations. This is what modern democracies, including ours, have been practicing for some time.

XI

THE CURSE OF THE DEBT

THE "RATIONALE" OF INFLATION

Does it matter how large the national debt is? Not really, quoting a widely used college textbook: "There is no sign that a high debt exhausts the credit of the government . . . and since as a last resort 'it can borrow from itself,' there need be no fear on this account."

When the national Treasury is unfathomably in the red, the nation turns color blind. It prefers to believe that red is black, or at least white, that liabilities, if not real assets, are "no burden." When this stage is reached, the doors of the fool's paradise open wide. Actually, the more indebted a nation is, the more immune it becomes from the fear of national bankruptcy. Once the principle that debts have to be repaid sooner or later is forgotten, all monetary inhibitions (which the discipline of the gold standard used to provide!) go with the political wind. The mileage of irresponsibility may be gauged by the Democratic platform of 1960 which promises *additional* expenditures of $80 billion for "rights-of-man" items in the next five years, as well as a few billions for increased military spending, all these on top of a current budget of $81 billion. For parallels in fiscal cynicism one has to go back to the days of the Jacobin-controlled French revolutionary convention.

A large debt *necessitates* money-printing and brings about price inflation. As it is, *debt monetization virtually is forced on the government by the colossal volume of the debt.* An attempt to collect, say, $100 billion savings for permanent investment in government bonds is out of the question. Interest rates would have to rise to prohibitive heights, and the flow of capital into mortgages, corporate and municipal bonds would have to be greatly reduced, if not stopped altogether. To avoid "excessive" interest rates and an excessive drain on the long-term funds, the Treasury is driven into the short-term money market. At this writing, $70-odd billion marketable obligations are maturing within one year. Another $48 billion nonmarketable bonds and $6 billion convertibles belong, in effect, in the same category, adding up to nearly one-half of the gross debt. Then, too, $73 billion marketables are due in one to five years, which is still a very short range.

To borrow short is very convenient—for financial charlatans. No problem of "placing" the bonds; most of the time, banks and others with excess cash can use three– to nine month treasury bills, one-year certificates, and similar instrumentalities. They are as good as cash and also yield a

AN INFLATION PRIMER

return. They are equivalent to cash because the government never defaults (how could it when it may, in effect, print the money with which to pay —"borrow from itself"), and there is a safe and secure outlet for them in the central bank. The Federal Reserve is here to pick up the slack, if any, and to turn it into legal tender. To monetize this kind of debt is a political *must*. Otherwise, not only the Treasury's credit but the entire credit structure would be doomed.

In final analysis, our credit system and our economic "security" rest on the national debt. Three-fifths of the Federal Reserve's assets consist of public securities. They also constitute most of the "cash" reserves of the corporations and savings and loan associations, and one-half to two-thirds of the banks' "liquidity." Virtually every cent of what we consider as prime liquid assets is either government paper or a claim on government paper.

FICTIONAL FINANCE AND MONETIZATION

The implications of this imaginary liquidity are devastating, as demonstrated by the behavior of the average banker. He finds that 40 per cent or more of his assets are "prime liquid," either paper money or claims on paper money to be issued against government paper. The purchasing power thus created has nothing to do with gold or silver or marketable goods or anything tangible, present or future. But his bank exudes "liquidity," as at no other time before 1934. Within very broad limits, he can proceed to make loans in almost any il-liquid fashion; legally and statistically, his situation remains comfortable and unassailable, provided he observes the customary rituals. It makes little difference how far the maturity of his business loans, mortgage loans and "other" loans is stretched; or how good the credit of the respective debtors is. He pours out installment credit by mortgaging the car and forgetting to check on the car's owner; he uses sight deposits to extend term loans (up to ten years) on oil-in-the-ground without a thought to the future price of overproduced oil; he finances construction that will pay its way only if the inflation continues indefinitely; he gives, and is encouraged to give, mortgage credit to young couples with or without secure jobs, at little or no down payment; and so on.

Financially, we live in a world of fiction, as we did in the 1920's. Then, a gigantic structure of stock-market values provided the fictitious liquidity that oiled the wheels of a mythical prosperity. Now, a gigantic structure of artificial bond values generates the lubricant of an equally fictitious prosperity—at mounting costs, prices and tensions—based on the implicit myth of the central bank's inexhaustible capacity to maintain, by debt monetization, the system's liquidity.

AN INFLATION PRIMER

The direct monetary consequences are patent. Suppose the Federal Reserve would suddenly refuse to buy, or to loan on, any more obligations of the national government (to say nothing of unloading an appreciable portion of its portfolio). The demand for those obligations could dry up overnight. Banks and financial institutions, business corporations, and many individuals would find themselves in a highly uncomfortable condition. Instead of swimming in liquidity, actual or potential, they might be faced with far-reaching liquidations. A scramble for "cash" could develop into an old-fashioned money panic. At any rate, security and real estate values, based as they are on the assumption of an indefinite credit flow, would be in for a severe beating.

But why should the Federal Reserve stop monetizing "whenever needed" to maintain the fiction of ample liquidity? And if it were reluctant, what would stop the Congress from forcing the central bank's hand? We do not doubt that the Congress is almighty, so far as legislation is concerned. The question is, merely, whether economic forces can be outlegislated. As things stand now, debt monetization by the Federal Reserve could not be resumed on a major scale without giving a fresh impetus to the vicious wage-price spiral, impairing the balance of payments, and sparking an outflow of gold. Unless we are ready to take another dollar devaluation on the chin, or to accept all-round price, wage, and foreign-exchange control—let alone the mass unemployment in the wake of a progressive inflation—the volume of Federal Reserve credit must be kept under control. And there is another Damocles sword hanging over the national economy, one that is being neglected, if not ignored, in the controversy about creeping inflation.

EXPANDING ON OVERDRAFT

Technically and psychologically, the inflated national debt is the pillar that holds up an over-inflated and rapidly growing structure of nonfederal (municipal, corporate, and individual) debts. That paper edifice is growing faster than the money volume or people's net income or net savings; faster than productive investment or industrial output. Totaling an estimated $603.1 billion at the end of 1959, the net private-plus-municipal debt is now three and one-half times what it was thirty years ago, when it collapsed by its own weight. But that ominous reminder does not tell the full story. What matters is the self-accelerating growth of the nonfederal debt tower. The addition in 1959 (*net*, after repayments) amounted to $57.4 billion, the largest ever, $7 billion more than in the previous peak year of 1957 and practically equaling its own increase in eight years of the booming twenties!

Patently, the growth of private, corporate, and

municipal debts—leaving aside the federal debt—finances our economic growth. It is equally patent that the one "growth" must not, and cannot, run far ahead of the other, for how could the debts be serviced and amortized, if not from the output of the investment which they financed? But the nonfederal debt zooms ahead of the GNP; at that, a large slice of the GNP consists of things (such as military hardware) and services (of bureaucrats, for example) which cost a lot but are not acceptable in payment to creditors.

Recourse on the national debt and its monetization is the built-in safeguard of the inflationist. Indeed, it is built into his mind. His is a mind equipped with statistics, dialectics, and wishfulness; it lacks nothing but foresight (and hindsight!). Living in a financial Eden, it ignores the serpent in the Garden. Its name is *overexpansion*.[1]

DEBT LIQUIDATION

With regard to nonfederal debts, unless the borrowing is done, in effect, for wasteful consumption or sheer gambling, and some of it surely is, the money serves to enlarge production and productive facilities. Directly or by indirection, credits (debts) provide the means of expanding the industrial capacity—from inventories and machines to buildings and plants—and an incentive to do so.

But the "leverage" in the financial setup of communities, corporations, and family budgets gets shorter and shorter, and we are heading for a devastating break of the dams which hold a *pernicious liquidation* from flooding the rampart of the economy. The crisis is unavoidable, as it was unavoidable in the past, when people awaken to the understanding that there are no real values, that is, earning power, back of the excessive capacities and malinvestments which their claims are supposed to represent.

Economic growth may be, and has been, fostered for years by a turbulent expansion of private and corporate debts. When the latter burst at the seams, *the government will not be able to step in* to save the day and maintain the growth. It may have no untapped tax sources left, and it will have exhausted its debt resources—overdrawn on its own credit. What remains is recourse on the central bank. By then, money printing may smooth the liquidation process, at best; at worst, it will bring about a run on the dollar. In either case, a period of economic stagnation is bound to be the reward for a prolonged process of capital erosion.

CREEPING INFLATION'S SUICIDE

Fortunately, there is salvation in prospect, nay, under way. The built-in automatism (a real one, not man-made) of the financial market place will terminate the reckless debt inflation. It does so by restraining the banks whose liquidity is impaired, with or without raising the interest rates. Rise they

AN INFLATION PRIMER

must, if the super-boom is rekindled, because the vast credit demand of the would-be debtors clashes with a growing reluctance of the capital owners and managers to invest in futility. Savings institutions are compelled to buy fixed-interest assets; individual savers may be bamboozled by solemn and meaningless assertions of maintaining artificial full employment and stability under the freely spending welfare state. Advocates of the welfare state ignore elementary economics: that full employment of a durable nature can be arrived at only if prices and costs adjust themselves to the market. But the necessary adjustments are postponed, if not stymied, by the inflation of debts.

Creeping inflation is a costly and dangerous luxury which only an economy that is *not* loaded with debts *as yet* can afford.

1. For an early consideration of this menace, see R. P. Ulin's "Are We Building Too Much Capacity?" *Harvard Business Review*, November–December, 1955.

XII

THE DOLLAR ON THE SICKBED

"GOOD AS GOLD"

The modern history of gold is rich in controversies. "Gold shortage and global devaluation" was the battle cry of the money cranks in the late twenties. Then, in the thirties, an excessive gold inflow sparked freakish proposals in the opposite direction, varying from an import tax on gold to its total demonetization. These proposals were answered on Friday, May 3, 1940, as follows:

For the excess of goods we shipped and for the dollar credits we granted we have taken gold in the last six years instead of promissory notes. The phrase "good as gold" still has real meaning in the world. I prefer the gold to pieces of foreign paper. I think most Americans agree with me.

The speaker was Mr. Morgenthau, FDR's Secretary of the Treasury. He would rank today as a right-wing Republican. His common-sense statement came virtually at the historic moment when common sense and American monetary policy parted company. In 1940, the dollar was indeed "good as gold" again. Since then, as a nation, we *take* neither gold nor promissory notes for the excess of goods we ship; instead, we *give* the foreigners our own promissory notes (dollar balances) as a sort of bonus; lately we "ship" out the gold, too. Nothing wrong with all that, indicated the Chairman of the Federal Reserve Board on February 24, *1960,* after the country had lost nearly $3½ billion of gold in two years. "Proper United States policy," he said, "could prevent any . . . 'hypothetical dilemma' [due to our continuous balance of payments deficits] from arising."

The dilemma to which the chairman was referring—the choice between losing our gold and restraining the inflation—is far from hypothetical or easily preventable. Actually, we are up against an explosive problem posed by the relentless growth of short-term dollar claims in the hands of foreigners and the simultaneous erosion of the gold reserve that is the coverage of last resort of a rapidly growing money supply. The candle of the dollar is burning at both ends.

THE SICK BALANCE OF PAYMENTS

The threat to the dollar is due to a persistent deficit in the country's international accounts. Our balance of trade with the outside world (merchandise and services, including tourist traffic, transportation, return on investments) produces an export surplus every year. Yet, for the last decade our *over-all balance of payments* showed a *deficit in every single year*—more payments due than receipts coming in.

Table A summarizes in the conventional fashion

TABLE A*
U.S. BALANCE OF PAYMENTS—WITHOUT GOLD AND FOREIGN CAPITAL MOVEMENTS
(Billions of Dollars)

	Trade Balance: Surplus of Exports or Imports (−) of Goods & Services	Unilateral Payments and Loans by U.S. Government & Privates (Net)	Surplus or Deficit (−)
1946	$ 7.8	$− 6.4	$1.4
1947	11.6	−10.6	1.0
1948	6.7	− 6.7	—
1949	6.4	− 7.0	−0.6
1950	2.3	− 6.0	−3.7
1951	5.2	− 6.2	−1.0
1952	4.9	− 6.7	−1.8
1953	4.7	− 7.3	−2.6
1954	5.0	− 6.7	−1.7
1955	4.4	− 6.3	−1.9
1956	6.5	− 8.6	−2.1
1957	8.2	− 8.9	−0.7
1958	4.6	− 8.4	−3.8
1959	1.9	− 8.4	−6.5

*Source, Tables A, B, and C: U.S. Department of Commerce, *Survey of Current Business*, July, 1954, and the June issues, 1955 to 1960.

the recent development of our international balance of payments, omitting the in-and-out movements of gold and of foreign capital. (They may be considered the balancing items, as we shall see.) It shows that billions more than the excess we earn businesswise is either given away by the government or lent out and remitted privately, in unilateral payments. But private investments and remittances abroad absorb only a small part of our trade surplus. What brings about the huge deficiency in the over-all balance is shown in Table B: the cornucopia of governmental handouts and military spending abroad.[1]

TABLE B
SOURCES OF DEFICIT ON U.S. FOREIGN ACCOUNTS
(Billions of Dollars)

Year	Net U.S. Government Handouts (Nonmilitary)	U.S. Military Spending Abroad (Net)	Total
1950	$ 3.7	$ 0.6	$ 4.3
1951	3.3	1.3	4.6
1952	2.5	2.0	4.5
1953	2.2	2.5	4.7
1954	1.8	2.5	4.3
1955	2.3	2.8	5.1
1956	2.5	3.0	5.5
1957	2.7	3.2	5.9
1958	2.8	3.4	6.2
1959	3.6	3.1	6.7
Total	27.4	24.4	51.8

DOLLARS IN OVERSUPPLY

By the end of 1959, the United States had lost $5 billion gold; exactly $5.264 billion since August, 1947. Another $0.526 billion left our gold reserve in the first eight and one-half months of 1960.

A fraction of the annual deficiency is accounted for by unaccounted items: "errors and omissions." Another fraction is covered by the net inflow of foreign long-term investments. But the main offsetting items are two: either we pay in internationally acceptable cash, which is gold; or the foreigners leave the money in the United States by acquiring bank balances and short-term treasury paper. What has actually happened is set out in Table C.

Three of every four "excess" dollars our govern-

THE DOLLAR ON THE SICK BED

TABLE C
U.S. BALANCE OF PAYMENTS DEFICIT AND OFFSETTING ITEMS
(Billions of Dollars)

Year	Gold Gain (−) or Loss*	Net Inflow of Foreign Capital	Statistical Errors and Omissions	Total Off-Setting Items	Balance of Payments Deficit (from Table A)
1950	$1.7	$1.9	†	$3.6	$ −3.7
1951	−0.1	0.6	0.5	1.0	−1.0
1952	−0.4	1.6	0.5	1.7	−1.8
1953	1.2	1.1	0.2	2.5	−2.6
1954	0.3	1.4	†	1.7	−1.7
1955	†	1.4	0.5	1.9	−1.9
1956	−0.3	1.8	0.6	2.1	−2.1
1957	−0.8	0.7	0.8	0.7	−0.7
1958	2.3	1.2	0.4	4.0	−3.8
1959	1.1	4.7	0.8	6.6	−6.5
Total	5.0	16.4			

*Gold "gain" means import of gold; hence minus sign.
†Less than 0.05.

ment dissipates abroad return like homing pigeons as claims on our gold reserve. At latest count (end of June, 1960) foreign-owned bank balances and short-term treasury securities amounted to $20.34 billion, having doubled in ten years. That is not all. American liquid assets, including currency, owned by foreigners other than banks and public authorities, may now stand around $2.4 billion. (The official estimate was $2.676 billion for 1957 and $2.522 billion for 1958.) Also, $2.3 billion of U.S. government notes and bonds with "original" maturities of more than one year are held by banks abroad and could be liquidated on fairly short notice. At this writing, the total of foreign-held liquid dollar assets is in the order of $25-odd billion (Table D).

AN INFLATION PRIMER

TABLE D*

End of Year	Foreign Liquid Assets† in U.S. (in millions)	U.S. Gold Reserve (in millions)	Ratio (%) of Foreign Claims to Gold
1949	$ 9,757	$24,563	39.7
1950	11,715	22,820	51.3
1957	18,593	22,857	81.3
1958	19,597	20,582	95.2
1959	23,723	19,507	121.6
Mid-1960	25,175	19,363	130.0
9/14/60	not available	18,939	n.a.

*Sources: U.S. Department of Commerce, *Survey of Current Business*, August, 1959, and June, 1960; *Federal Reserve Bulletin*, August, 1960.

†Including U.S. government securities with original maturities of more than one year and estimated foreign nonbank holdings of American liquid assets.

The outer world's dollar shortage (that was to last forever, remember?) turned into an oversupply of dollars abroad. This is a unique situation: a country deliberately and systematically squanders its gold reserve and piles up a mountain of "hot-money" obligations of the most volatile sort, though it does not wish to impair the gold value of its currency. To make things worse, the Federal Reserve deliberately lowers its discount rates to foster domestic inflation—and the gold outflow.

CAN THE BALANCE OF PAYMENTS BE REDRESSED?

The give-away programs are a built-in feature of our national policy. In the official theory, they are a *must* for the cold war. Why they have to total an annual $8 to $9 billion, rather than $5 billion or $11 billion, has never been explained. The standards, if any, by which the volume of this fantastic subsidy (to the special interests in exports) is determined, are seemingly divorced from any concern about the balance of payments, the gold stock, or the stability of the dollar.

There is scant likelihood that our balance of trade should improve greatly and in a lasting fashion. The huge surpluses of the early post-1945 era (Table A) are out of the question since Europe's and Japan's recovery. Their competitive prowess makes itself felt sharply along innumerable lines of merchandise. It is greatly strengthened by operations under American licenses and by the exodus of American firms in search of more profiitable climates. If our exports have risen this this year (1960) as against last, it is largely because of the coincidence of a domestic slowdown with a superboom abroad. However, unit cost differentials still tend to broaden in our disfavor, due to the effect of (American-financed) technological progress abroad, combined with much lower wages there than on this side. Once the cyclical slowdown reaches Europe, as it well may, and non-recurrent factors fade out,[2] European exports will increase and their imports from the United States will decline.

Two-fifths of our exports consist of raw commodities and semimanufactured items, the weakest links in the world price structure. Foodstuff imports are restrained everywhere; the unloading of farm surpluses (unless in exchange for payment in irredeemable currencies) is up against severe obstacles. Most industrial staple prices are depressed; a moderate recession in Europe would bring them down further. There is no hope for an early revival of our coal, petroleum, and metal exports which accounted for more than half the 1958–59 shrinkage in our total exports.

As to economizing on imports, a severe domestic recession would do, ironically. Higher tariffs and restrictive quotas would not do; they run counter to the national policy of fostering international trade and would boomerang in higher domestic costs and fewer exports. At that, Washington nods to European "integration" movements, although their result is to discriminate against our exports.

In its embarrassment, the U.S. government pressures the Allies, especially Germany, to "play the game" and chip in with credits to the underdeveloped nations. This the Allies do, on a moderate scale. What they contribute (mostly in their own "backyards") means an addition to, rather than a substitute for, our aid. The discussion about tying our aid directly to our exports has died down; it would not solve the problem anyway. Shifting a major part of the cost of maintaining U.S. garrisons in the host countries may discourage their own armament efforts.

THE DOLLAR ON THE SICK BED

Foreign governments may be persuaded to accelerate payments on their long-term debts to the United States. They are making advance payments. Evidently, the effect could only be minor. If feasible at all, an attempt to discourage foreign central banks from withdrawing gold would most certainly boomerang.

Theoretically, recourse could be taken to American investments abroad, at least on the "liquid" assets amounting to $5.6 billion (end of 1958); the government owns $2.14 billion. How much could be liquidated—risking an international panic—is open to question. Uncle Sam did borrow from the International Monetary Fund, but he will have to repay sooner or later. Such stratagems are helpful in a short-lived emergency only. That is not what we are up against. In fact, the dollar predicament is to continue indefinitely. Presently, foreigners could claim some 30 per cent more gold than we possess. How imminent is the menace that they might?—bearing in mind that international trade and finance, the domestic price structure, in fact the whole *economic system,* are intimately *linked to gold* and its present dollar price.

1. Military transfers under grants, consisting of weapons, etc., are not included among the unilateral payments, and they do not affect the balance of payments.
2. A temporary upsurge of European demand for cotton, aluminum, and airplanes, and the "upward adjustment" of our cotton and wheat subsidies, are primarily responsible for the rise of the "visible" trade balance by nearly $2 billion in the first half of 1960. Merchandise exports are likely to increase in a recession.

XIII

THE SAD PREDICAMENT OF THE FOOL'S PARADISE

HEADING FOR INSOLVENCY

"We—you and I and our Government—must avoid the impulse to live only for today, plundering for our own ease and convenience, the precious resources of tomorrow.

"We cannot mortgage the material assets of our grandchildren without risking the loss also of their potential and spiritual heritage. We want democracy to survive for all generations to come, not to become the insolvent phantom of tomorrow."

These were the memorable farewell words of President Eisenhower. Unfortunately, it took nearly eight years before his administration discovered that the country is up against an impending balance-of-payment crisis. There is nothing "impending" about it any longer. It will not take eight months, possibly not even eight weeks, before the incoming Kennedy administration will have to take drastic steps—and, especially, to leave out some it was planning to take—in order to cope with that crisis.

As these lines go to press, the problem has reached the critical stage. We have lost in less than three years over $5.2 billion of our gold reserve (closer to $6 billion, including the gold borrowed from the International Monetary Fund), more than $2 billion in the last four months to mid-January, 1961.

Where are the surplus dollars coming from, to be turned into gold by redemption at the Federal Reserve Bank of New York or by purchasing gold on the London, Toronto, and other markets? Our balance of payments is "leaking" in several places, through which dollar claims are flowing out in excessive quantities: $3.3 billion in 1958, over $5 billion in 1959, an estimated $3.5 to $4 billion "only" in 1960.

A temporary leak was created by the Federal Reserve System itself. Since early 1960 it has irresponsibly lowered and kept low the short-term money rates, thereby creating a broad-yield differential between foreign and domestic credit instruments. The result was a great deal of American capital flow to London and Frankfurt. However, since the European central banks willy-nilly reduced their discount rates (in order to please the Americans), the differential has been cut to a point where it scarcely covers the costs involved in transferring short-term funds from these shores to the others.

Potentially far more important is a second leak: flight from the dollar. At home and abroad, people have come to suspect that the dollar will be

THE SAD PREDICAMENT OF THE FOOL'S PARADISE

devalued. A rational reaction is, for the foreigner: to get rid of his dollars; for the American: to hedge by buying gold or gold certificates, possibly even on money borrowed abroad (on 97 per cent margin). But the total of such transactions has been, so far, the proverbial drop in the bucket. Mr. Eisenhower's order to liquidate gold holdings held abroad affects residents of this country only; it could scarcely be policed.[1] In any case, it amounts to fighting the smoke, rather than the fire that produces the smoke. The run on the dollar is not caused by the run on the dollar; it is caused by lack of trust in our willingness to defend the dollar, to overcome the persistent deficit in our balance of payments.

EROSION—HOW MUCH LONGER?

That brings us to the decisive "holes" from which the deterioration of the payments balance and the consequent gold outflow stems. They are: directly, the lavishment of governmental expenditures abroad, totaling between $8 billion and $9 billion a year; indirectly, the domestic cost-price inflation. The latter reduces the export prowess of American business, fosters the emigration of American plants, and generates excessive imports.

If our private consumption is "conspicuous," as we are being told, it is because of unreasonable taxation and of inflation fears that induce reckless spending and purely speculative investing. As

130

to our ability to compete, we formerly led the world in technological progress. Where we are presently, after many years of spoon-fed "growth," was aptly summarized by the *Wall Street Journal:*

Frequently shoddy workmanship. Crippling strikes for whimsical reasons. Disdain for the contract. The enormous economic toll of featherbedding which is rapidly turning this into a high-cost economy, as reflected in the inability of U.S. products to compete, as once they did, in world markets. Perhaps most important of all, the erosion of values once held high.

... if there is softness in America today it is not primarily inferior education or "inadequate" public spending but this union and statist sponsored philosophy of indolence.

The problem is more than economic, it is moral. For what we are witnessing on every side is not only the financial disintegration of governments. We are witnessing the collapse of individual responsibility.

Reduced exports and high imports, on top of the "political" dollar flow, add up to an abundance of dollar balances and claims in foreign hands. They are claims on gold, in the ratio of an ounce of gold of 9/10ths fineness to each $35. How long can the creditors feel assured that their claims are really worth the gold if the pile of claims—over $27 billion already, with the gold reserve down to $17.5 billion—keeps rising at a *daily* rate of well over $10 million? Presently, the central banks of the industrial nations (Europe, Canada, Japan) refrain, as a rule, from withdraw-

THE SAD PREDICAMENT OF THE FOOL'S PARADISE

ing dollar funds they had accumulated on this side. But of the funds they acquire from here on, about 75 per cent is being converted into gold. Naturally, they cannot indefinitely tie up in dollar balances their ultimate liquidity reserves while the dollar's convertibility is not assured. Their monetary sovereignty, the freedom to act with some degree of financial independence, is at stake. As it is, they cannot help but consider dollar reserves as a permanent "investment," of which no major fraction could be withdrawn without sparking a panic on, and the collapse of, the dollar.

Our problem, then, is to cut the cloth to the size of the figure—to *hold the deliberate outpour of funds within the limits set by the surplus* produced through current (commercial) transactions with the outer world. As to bolstering that commercial surplus, there is one effective way, one only: *balance the budget and stop the monetization of the national debt* by the Federal Reserve System.

AT THE END OF CREEPING INFLATION'S ROPE

With their eyes riveted on the gross national product and similar "aggregate" concoctions, the addicts of managed money and creeping inflation ignore the "golden rule" of a free society. It is this: If you overstrain your financial system, you lose your gold. Gold, pooh-poohed by the pseudo-liberals as a "barbaric relic," is the ultimate regulator that keeps the economic world in balance. Gold is the governor that restrains the credit apparatus from expanding wildly and the welfare states from running headlong into collectivism, if not into ruthless tyranny.

The attraction and virtues of gold are that governments can't roll it off or create it with the stroke of a pen. It imposes some monetary discipline by affording a safeguard, a store of value which may escape looting, debasement and other forms of spoliation.

That is why the people of the East, with centuries of experience of rascality by rulers, bandits and other depredators on human welfare, hoard a few pieces of gold against the days of pillage and spoliation. That is why the supposedly enlightened peoples of the West have to tie their money systems in some way to a real commodity, acquired by an expensive and ugly outlay of human toil.

And it is precisely because governments in our time have grossly debauched the currency that they now hope to cover up the distortions by manipulating the price of gold. George Schwartz, "Really Cheap Money," *The Sunday Times,* London, November 13, 1960.

There is no escape from the rule of gold, except by taking national insolvency on the chin, which is what dollar devaluation means. Raising the dollar price of gold would be the signal to devalue all currencies—global inflation with all-round, semi-totalitarian controls over international transactions, domestic prices, profits, and wages.

It would be the greatest irony of history, and an unparalleled tragedy for western civilization, if America, by *exporting inflation,* would force the

THE SAD PREDICAMENT OF THE FOOL'S PARADISE

world back into the commercial and monetary chaos from which it has been slowly emerging—wiping out the stabilization, for the sake of which the American taxpayer has spent a round $80 billion since World War II. At that point, inevitably rising prices would make illusory all (alleged) advantages resulting from a boost of the gold price and would call for more of the same fake medicine. And it would mean a thorough defeat in the cold war, with the material, political, and prestige advantages accruing to the Soviets.

1. Little New Zealand, an island country, tries hard but does not succeed in stopping gamblers from transferring domestic funds with which to play in Australian lotteries, Irish sweepstakes, and British football pools.

APPENDIX

MONEY SUPPLY AND INFLATION

WHAT IS MONEY SUPPLY?

The collectivist propensity to invent fresh arguments in order to justify ever more inflation is something to behold. A latest sample is the complaint that we are suffering from deflation: in the twelve-month period to the end of May, 1960, the money supply—meaning the sum of currency outside the banks and adjusted net demand deposits in the banks—has declined by $3 billion, or 2.5 per cent. So, let's hurry and print more money. The facts are, however, that during the current (alleged) decline of the money supply the net volume of outstanding debts rose by $50 billion or more, bank loans increased by $12 billion, or almost 10 per cent, and the consumer price index went up by 2 per cent.

Just what is the money supply—supply of what? At stake is the definition of money, a bitterly fought issue for centuries. Monetary policies were built on arbitrary definitions, ranging from the eighteenth century doctrine (David Hume) that all credit instruments are money, even bonds and shares of common stocks, to the dogma underlying the Peel's Bank Charter Act of 1844 that only gold coins and Bank of England notes were to be counted. Presently, there is virtual agreement that the concept has to be broader than the latter definition and narrower than the former, still leaving a wide range of "freedom" for arbitrary choice.

Of course, the choice of a definition depends on the functional purpose it is supposed to serve. What we want to know is the volume of all media of exchange, and of claims on the same, that are or may become effective demand for goods and services. Accordingly, we have to include not only the "active" money in process of being turned over during a chosen period but also all other instruments which might be used for payment, even if they are "idle" at the time.

ALL DEPOSITS ARE MONEY

What, then, is the justification for using the figure of cash-plus-demand-deposits as the measure of the money supply, excluding the time and savings deposits—as it is customary in Europe? None whatsoever, unless it is sheer convenience. True, checking accounts have a higher "velocity of circulation" than savings accounts.[1] But the latter do turn around; withdrawals amount to 60 per cent or more of incoming payments. Savings accounts are subject to a mere 30 days' notice provision, which is not being enforced; they serve also as a base for "pyramiding" deposits. This is implicitly recognized by the law that prescribes mandatory minimum-liquidity reserves for all kinds of bank deposits, except those of the government, considering them as "idle" purchasing power. (The banks hold an equal amount of government securities against government deposits.)

The *Federal Reserve Bulletin's* monthly tabulation of the monetary and banking system's Consolidated Conditions includes under "deposits adjusted and currency" all so-called time deposits (an improper designation). But savings and loan associations are omitted on the grounds, presumably, that they are not banks in the legal terminology. Yet, their "savings capital"—that grows at an annual rate of $6 to $7 billion (!)—is no different in monetary character from savings deposits in banks, though not subject to statutory *cash* reserve requirements. Nor are these deposits turned over at a much lower rate. True, there is no legal obligation to redeem them on demand. But they are being paid out, and the owners regard them as equivalent to cash.

In their own minds, *money is what people consider as purchasing power,* available at once or shortly. People's "liquidity" status and financial dispositions are not affected by juristic subtilities and technicalities. One kind of deposit is as good as another, provided it is promptly redeemable into legal tender at virtual face value and is accepted in settling debts. The volume of total demand for goods and services is not affected by the distribution of purchasing power among the diverse reservoirs into which that purchasing power is placed. As long as free transferability obtains from one reservoir to the other, the deposits cannot differ in function or value.

SAVINGS AND SEMANTICS

For the decision to buy a home it is irrelevant whether the money needed for down payment is held in a bank, in a savings institution, or in a safe box. The "money supply" is available in any case.

A source of confusion is the identification of savings deposits with savings. The former are no more and no less "saved" than are the funds put on a checking account or the currency held in stockings. In all three cases, someone is refraining from consumption (for the time being); in all three, the funds constitute actual purchasing power. And it makes no difference in this context how the purchasing power is generated originally: dug out of a gold mine, "printed" by a governmental agency, or "created" by a bank loan. As a matter of fact, savings banks and associations do exactly what commercial banks do: they build a credit structure on fractional reserves. They do so even more "effectively" than the commercial banks, due to the higher reserve requirements for demand deposits.

AN INFLATION PRIMER

The fact alone that for credit expansion the commercial banks indiscriminately utilize all deposited funds, whether on demand or on savings accounts, should dispel the semantic confusion caused by the ambivalent use of the term "savings."

POTENTIAL MONEY

But then, are all claims on stated sums of currency to be considered as parts of the money supply? Or where is the line to be drawn? As in most matters human, there is no cut-and-dried line of demarcation. There are numerous shades of transition from money to non-money. It all depends on the circumstances which determine the judgment of the market place. Everything is money, to repeat, that is usable as such or is readily monetizable. That brings us to the "potential" money supply.

The actual money supply, whether active or idle, consists of legal tender and its substitutes. But there are credit instruments which, though not directly usable to make payments, can be turned at all times and *without loss of capital* into active purchasing power. Bankers' acceptances, high-class commercial paper and "street loans" were used for this function at one time or another. Since 1934, treasury securities of not more than one-year lifetime (bills, notes, certificates) have taken over the function on an unprecedented scale.

They are alternatives to cash, having ready market as interest-yielding near-demand deposits which cannot go in default—if only because the central bank is expected to monetize them, in ultimate resort. (This is implicit in its policy of maintaining an "orderly market" for government obligations.) Thereby, they become equivalents of money and a temporary repository of major funds in the hands of the public.

At the end of last May about $45.4 billion of short (up to one year) treasuries, or $21 billion more than five years earlier, was held by nonbank investors. They are primeliquid assets, in the market's opinion, just like bank balances, because they can be turned into cash on short notice. Liquidation before maturity may cause a loss if the interest rate has risen after the purchase; but the owners either do not contemplate such premature liquidation or expect to be compensated by the return they had earned in the meantime.

Funds are being shifted from deposits into short treasuries, and vice versa; in the process, the volume of demand deposits appears to undergo a deflation, or the opposite. Which is what happened recently. As customers depleted their accounts in order to buy federal short maturities, the "money supply" in terms of currency-plus-demand-deposit has contracted for the simple reason that the banks used the proceeds from the sale of treasury securities to reduce their debts at the federal reserve banks. But of course, the total money volume—actual and potential combined—was not affected.

"LIQUIDITY" VERSUS MONEY SUPPLY

The question at stake is not to find a definition suitable for the textbooks. The question is: to determine the "dimension" relevant for monetary policy. As the (British) Radcliffe Report put it cogently:

> The immediate object of monetary action is to affect the level of total demand.
> Monetary action works upon total demand by altering the liquidity position of financial institutions and of firms and people desiring to spend on real resources; the *supply of money* itself *is not the critical factor.* [Italics ours.] *Committee on the Working of the monetary System Report,* London, August, 1959, p. 135.

The conventional money-supply notion is totally unsatisfactory, even misleading, as a quantitative base for the understanding (forecasting?) of price-level trends and for the guidance of monetary policy. In this country, as in Britain, the central bank's attempts to check the inflation are to a large extent, if not altogether, frustrated by the unwieldy volume of overhanging "liquidity."

A classic case of the thoughtless application of a conventional concept has been provided by the economists of the International Monetary Fund. In 1952, they announced with fanfares that the Western world's inflation troubles were over—

MONEY SUPPLY AND INFLATION

prices *have* caught up with the inflated "money supply." They forgot all about the vast volume of monetizable public debt almost everywhere. The dismal record of that forecast did not inhibit Per Jacobsson, the IMF's managing director, to come out lately with the same wishful statement that "wartime inflation" *has* come to an end and price stability *has* returned to the free world.

This is not the first time that Mr. Jacobsson has expressed such unwarranted optimism. As head of the Bank for International Settlements, he made the following statement in the 1954–55 Annual Report of that institution (p. 80): "It seems, indeed, very likely that, provided the world remains at peace, the inflationary phase of post-war economic development has now come to an end." A more realistic application of the concept appears in the August, 1960, *Monthly Review* of the Federal Reserve Bank of Atlanta. The comment (without reference to Mr. Jacobsson) is: "Has the economic environment changed so much that the money supply is no longer excessive as it was in most of the post-war period? He who would give a firm answer to this question at this point would be foolhardy, indeed."

1. Actually, a large, but statistically unknown, portion of demand deposits is permanently inactive. Currency, too, is being "hoarded" in substantial volume. Yet the "idle purchasing media" are generally counted as part of the active money supply. Compare the June, 1957, *Special Bulletin* of the American Institute for Economic Research, Great Barrington, Mass.

BIBLIOGRAPHY:
A SELECTION

Adams, Walter, and Gray, Horace M. *Monopoly in America.* New York: Macmillan Company, 1955.

Backman, Jules. *Wage Determination—An Analysis of Wage Criteria.* Princeton, N.J.: D. Van Nostrand Co., Inc., 1959.

Bauer, Peter T., and Yamey, Basil S. *The Economics of Underdeveloped Countries.* Chicago: University of Chicago Press, 1957.

Bell, J. W., and Spahr, W. E. (eds.). *A Proper Monetary and Banking System for the United States.* New York: Ronald Press Co., 1960.

Briefs, Götz. *Unionism Reappraised.* Washington, D.C.: American Enterprise Association, 1960.

Brown, A. J. *The Great Inflation 1939-1951.* London: Oxford University Press, 1955.

Chamberlin, Edward H. *The Economic Analysis of Labor Union Power.* Washington, D.C.: American Enterprise Association, 1958.

Fisher, Robert Moore. *Twenty Years of Public Housing.* New York: Harper & Brothers, 1959.

Harwood, E. C. *Cause and Control of the Business Cycle.* 5th ed. Great Barrington, Mass.: American Institute for Economic Research, 1957.

Hazlitt, Henry. *The Failure of the 'New Economics': An Analysis of the Keynesian Fallacies.* Princeton, N.J.: D. Van Nostrand Co., Inc., 1959.

Kriz, Miroslav A. *Gold in World Monetary Affairs Today.* ("Essays in International Finance," No. 34.) Princeton, N.J.: Princeton University Press, 1959.

Lester, R. A. *As Unions Mature.* Princeton, N.J.: Princeton University Press, 1959.

Lindblom, C. E. *Unions and Capitalism.* New Haven, Conn.: Yale University Press, 1949.

McCaleb, W. F. *How Much Is a $?* San Antonio, Tex.: Naylor Co., 1959.

Nussbaum, A. *A History of the Dollar.* New York: Columbia University Press, 1957.

Petro, Sylvester. *Power Unlimited—The Corruption of Union Leadership.* New York: Ronald Press Co., 1959.

Poirot, Paul L. *The Pension Idea.* Irvington-on-Hudson, N.Y.: Foundation for Economic Education, Inc., 1950.

Pound, Roscoe. *Labor Unions and the Concept of Public Service.* Washington, D.C.: American Enterprise Association, 1959.

Röpke, Wilhelm. *Humane Economy.* Chicago: Henry Regnery Co., 1960.

Schlesinger, James R. *The Political Economy of National Security.* New York: Frederick A. Praeger, Inc., 1960.

Spahr, Walter E. *An Appraisal of the Monetary Policies of Our Federal Government, 1933–1938.* New York: Economists' National Committee on Monetary Policy, 1938.

———. *The Case for the Gold Standard.* New York: Economists' National Committee on Monetary Policy, 1940.

———. *It's Your Money.* New York: Economists' National Committee on Monetary Policy, 1946.

Terborgh, George. *Corporate Profits in the Decade 1947–1956.* Washington, D.C.: Machinery and Allied Products Institute, 1957.

Torff, Selwyn H. *Collective Bargaining: Negotiations and Agreements.* New York: McGraw-Hill Book Company, Inc., 1953.

Velie, Lester. *Labor U.S.A.* New York: Harper & Brothers, 1959.

White, Andrew D. *Fiat Money Inflation in France.* New York: Appleton Co., 1896.

Wiggins, James W., and Schoeck, Helmut. *Foreign Aid Reexamined.* Washington, D.C.: Public Affairs Press, 1958.

Winder, George. *A Short History of Money.* London: Newman Neame, Ltd., 1959.

Wright, David M. *The Creation of Purchasing Power.* London: Cambridge University Press, 1942.

INDEX

INDEX

Adams, W., and Gray, H. M...55
Administered prices 50-51, 55
"Aggregates" 132
American Institute for
   Economic Research .5, 142, 144
Anthracite 49
Anti-capitalistic sentiment,
   source of 80-82
Austerity 82, 93

Backman, Jules 144
Balance of payments. 120-127, 128
Balance of trade...120-21, 125-26
Bank examiners 107
Banking system ......·10, 106-8
Bank for International
   Settlements 142
Bank portfolios 106-8
Bank reserves 14-15, 137
Bankruptcy (default) 92-93,
                    109, 133
Bauer, Peter, and
   Yamey, B. S. 144
Bell, J. W., and Spahr,
   Professor Walter E........144
"Big" business 50-51
"Bills only" 22
Bolshevism 76-77, 79-83, 99
Boulding, K. E. 37
Briefs, Professor Gotz.......144
Brokers' loans 96, 139
Brown, Professor A. J........144
Brown, E. H. P., and
   Hopkins, S. V. 70
Budget, unbalanced 85
Budgetary controls 102
Bureaucracy,
   bureaucratism 80-81, 85
Business cycles,
   "rationale" of 63-67
Business standards,
   deterioration of 55, 131

Capacity to pay 45-47
Capital
   flight 129-30
   gains 55
Capitalism
   people's 94-97
   rationale of 65

shortcomings of 63-64, 81
Central banking (see also:
Federal Reserve)
   inflation and freedom....59-60
Chamberlin, Professor
   Edward H. 144
Clayton Act 50
Cold war, defeat in..........134
Collectivism 56, 64,
                77-82, 100, 135
*Commercial and Financial
   Chronicle* 70, 72
Competition 59, 77
(see also: price mechanism; monopoly)
   international 125-26
Consumer debt 89-94
Consumption,
   "conspicuous" 64, 130
Contracyclical policies ...34, 41,
                    62-63
Corruption 77-78
Cortney, Philip 83
Cost of living................8
   cutting 66-67
   of construction 91
Credit
   controls 14-15, 95-96
   creation of 10-17, 20
   expansion by government 26-27, 34
   qualitative. 11-12, 14, 64-65, 102
Crossman, Richard 82

Debts (see also: public debt;
monetization; credit)
   burden of 6, 94, 98-109
   business 94
   debt management 22-27
   income and 89-92, 97, 103
   inflation of 87-88
   liquidation of 116-17
   mortgage .88-89, 91-92, 97, 113
   municipal 115-16
   personal 88-92, 97
Deficit finance 28
Deposit insurance 105-6
Deposits, pyramiding of...137-39
Depreciation of purchasing power
(*see* inflation)

147

INDEX *(continued)*

Depressions 37, 63-68, 89, 93
Devaluation 60, 114, 129-30, 133-34
Discount rate policy.........129
Dollar "shortage" 124
Douglas, Senator Paul H......61

Eccles, Mariner S.............39
Economic system 77
Economist, The (London)..61, 99
Eisenhower, President ..128, 130
"Elastic currency" 21-22
Employment Act (1946).......78
Erosion of standards......130-32
Escalators 36
"Eternal prosperity" 94

Farm subsidies 34, 41, 53
Featherbedding 38, 45, 131
Federal Reserve System....15-17, 18-27, 39-40, 94, 129, 132
  freedom of 105
Financial disintegration 131
Fiscal legerdemains 103-5
First National City Bank
  (New York) 55
Fisher, Robert Moore 144
"Flexibility" 23
"Fools paradise" 128-34
Foreign aid 53, 121, 124-25, 130, 134
Freedom, meaning of 57-60
Fringe benefits 30, 44, 45
Full employment 34, 63, 77-78, 98-99, 118

Galbraith, Professor J.
  Kenneth 73, 82
Gambling (*see* speculation)
General Motors 42
"Gold inflation" 3
Gold price (*see* devaluation)
Gold
  dollar balances and 122-24
  loss of..120, 123, 128-29, 131-32
  requirement 21
  role of....119, 122, 127, 132-33
  standard 21, 56-57, 76
Gray, Horace M., and
  Adams, W. 55

Greenbacks 6
Grievance procedures 38
"Growth"
  balanced 68
  debts and 117
  ideology of 57, 81
  rate of 83, 84-87
  vs. progress 65-70, 84-87, 93

Hazlitt, Henry 144
Hoarding 142
Hopkins, S. V., and
  Brown, E. H. P.............70
Home ownership 91, 97
Housing, subsidized.51, 52, 92-93
Hume, David 135

Illiquidity 59, 88, 108, 113
Industrial conflicts 32-33, 44-45, 49, 131
Inflation (*see also:* monetization; debts; money supply)
  anti-capitalism and 95
  built-in 35-38, 110
  burden of..........5-6, 48-49
  "cost-push" 30-36
  creeping 1-2, 4-8, 71-83, 85, 94-95, 117-18, 130, 132-34
  criminality and 33, 97
  debt management 20-27
  definition of 2-3, 54
  employer resistance and..53-54
  "exported" 133-34
  fixed return assets and 5
  freedom and 59-60, 81-82
  galloping 1-2, 7, 20
  global 133-34
  hedges 36
  ideology of 98-100, 110-12
  income and 2-6, 48-49, 78-79, 81, 86-87
  "legalized robbery"....2-3, 5-6
  "modus operandi" 10-17, 28, 34, 36
  over-expansion and 66, 68-69, 88
  perpetual 57
  psychology 95, 97
  source of 18-27, 28-29, 33-34, 141

148

INDEX *(continued)*

speculation and 7-8, 95-97
taxation and 6-7, 48
Inflationists 56-57, 61-64, 69, 78-82, 84, 116, 118, 135
Instability, built in 89
Intelligentsia, "liberal" 35
Interest rates, ...93, 94, 99-100
International Monetary Fund 127, 129, 141-42
Inventory cycles........64, 65-66
Investment cycles 65-66
Investment trusts 95-96

Jacobsson, Per 142
Jacoby, Professor N. H........92

Kennedy administration 128
Keynes, John Maynard.62, 71, 82
Keynesians 64
Kriz, Miroslav A. 144

Labor
  costs 30-35, 48-49
  disincentives 44-45
  incentives 44
  legislation 38
  monopoly 32-35
  shortage 34
Labour Party 82
Laissez-faire 56-61, 68
Laws, economic 56
Legal tender 18
Lester, Professor R. A.......144
Lewis, John L. 49
Liberals, self-styled 49, 81-82
Lindblom, Professor C. E....144
Liquidation of debts.........109
Liquidity 14-15, 66, 107-8, 141-42
  fictitious 113
"Listed" prices 51
Lobbies *(see* pressure groups)

Mal-investments 36
Managed money 20-22, 77
Margin requirements 96
Martin, Chairman W. McChesney 24-25, 120
Marx, Karl (Marxism)........63
Military spending abroad 121, 126

Mills, F. C.............67-68, 70
Minimum prices 41
Mobility 91
Monetary discipline 22-23
Monetary expansion...25-26, 135
Monetary velocity...........136
Monetization, inflationary .12-17, 35, 93, 98-99, 111-16, 132, 139-40
Money
  active 136, 139
  definition of 135-37
  idle 136-37
  potential 139-41
"Money shortage" 64
Money supply 8-9, 35, 135-42
Monopolies 50-52, 55, 58
(see labor)
Morgenthau, Secretary of Treasury 119

National income (product) 84-5, 88-90
New Deal 95
New York Times 66
New Zealand 134

Oligopoly 50-51
Open Market Committee.....18
Open Market operations 19-20, 25
Over-expansion *(see* inflation)
Over-loaning 27, 88
Over-the-counter market 96

Paper money *(see* managed money)
Patronage 77-78, 80
Patronage State 76
Patterson, R. T..............70
Peel's Bank Charter Act.....135
Perpetual prosperity 60-63
Petro, Professor Sylvester....145
"Philosophy" of inflation..56-70
Planning 81, 84
Pound, Dean Roscoe 145
Power vs. freedom 64, 76-82
Pressure groups (lobbies) 33-35, 52, 81
Price level 30-31, 47, 70

149

INDEX *(continued)*

stability 61-63
Price mechanism ... 41-42, 51, 55, 59, 77, 80-81, 93-94, 117
Price supports 51
Procurement, military 51
Productivity .. 31-32, 42-47, 66-67
Profit inflation 7-8, 49-55
Protectionism 51, 53, 126
Public debt
   burden of 98-109, 110-12
   ceiling over 22
   economic effects of 100-3
   inflation and 28-29, 100
   "roll over" of 105
   "wealth creation" by 98-99

Radcliffe Report 141
Rationality, economic 58
Recessions 37
Reserve requirements
   for banks 20-22
Reynaud, Paul 2
"Right to work" 33, 42
Risk-bearing and profits 65
Roepke, Professor
   Wilhelm 97, 145
Roosevelt, President F. D. 98
Rueff, Jacques 83

Samuelson, Professor
   Paul A., ... 72
Savings
   bonds 41
   deposits 138
   erosion of 5-6, 54-55
   institutions . 17, 88, 106, 137-40
Schlesinger, Professor
   James R. 145
Schwartz, George (London) .. 133
Securities and
   Exchange Commission .. 96, 107
Sherman Act 50
Slichter, Professor S. H. 82
Smith, Adam 102
Social security 41, 104-5
Spahr, Professor

Walter E., and
   Bell, J. W. 145
Speculators .7, 66, 95-96, 130, 134
Spirals, wage-price 28-38
"Stabilizers" 41
Stockpiling 51
Strikes *(see* industrial conflicts)
Subsidies 34, 41, 48-49, 51, 85
Sweden 79
Switzerland 79

Tax avoidance (evasion) 7
Tax burden 6-7, 49-50
Teamsters Union 33
Terborgh, George 145
Trade unions ... 32-33, 39-41, 46, 49-50, 52-55, 75
Treasury—Federal
   Reserve cooperation 23-25

Unemployment 37
   technological 48
Union shop 42
United Automobile
   Workers 33

Velie, Professor Lester 145
Viner, Professor Jacob 71

Wage claims,
   justification of 45-47
Wage structure 47
Wages *(see* labor costs;
   inflation; productivity)
   guaranteed 41
Wall Street Journal 41
War finance 6
Welfare State
   (welfarism) 76, 95, 118
White, Andrew D. 145
Work rules *(see* featherbedding)
Wright, Professor
   David McCord 145

Yamey, B. S., and
   Bauer, Peter 144